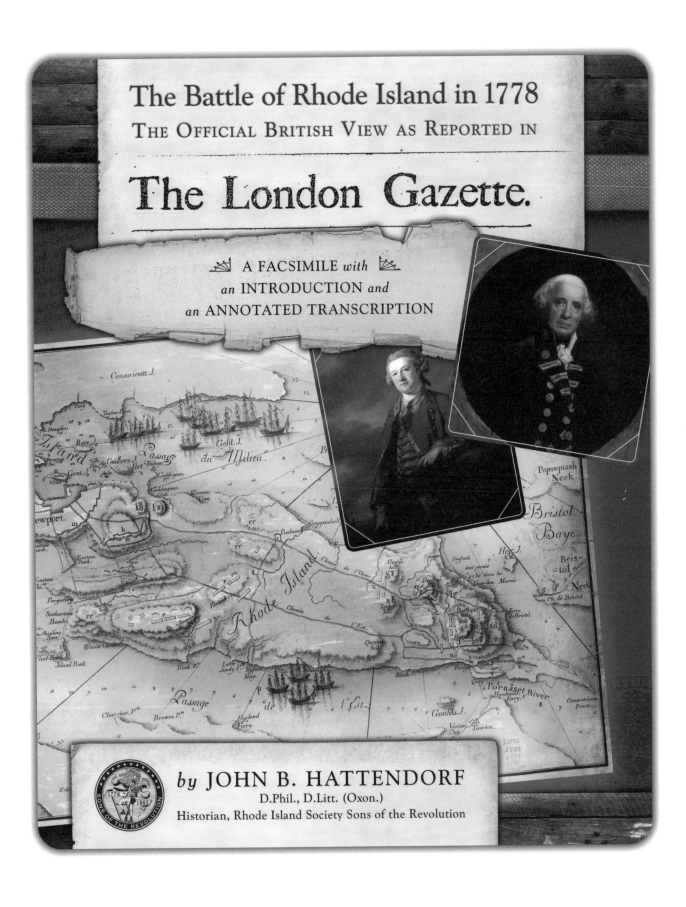

The Battle of Rhode Island in 1778
THE OFFICIAL BRITISH VIEW AS REPORTED IN

The London Gazette.

A FACSIMILE *with*
an INTRODUCTION *and*
an ANNOTATED TRANSCRIPTION

by **JOHN B. HATTENDORF**
D.Phil., D.Litt. (Oxon.)
Historian, Rhode Island Society Sons of the Revolution

Plan de Rhode Island

et les differentes Operations de la flotte =
= françoises et des Troupes Americaines commandées
par le Major General Sullivan contre les forces
de Terre et de Mer des Angloïs depuis le 9 Aoust
Jusqu'à la nuit du 30 au 31 du meme mois 1778 que
les Americains ont fait leur retraites

a Forts . . . . Construits par les Angloïs et évacués la nuit du 8 au 9 Aoust, après
b, c, d, e, f. Redoutes l'Entrée de la flotte, aux Ordres de M.r le Co.te d'Estaing, dans
g Redans . . . . . . le Canal du Milieu.
h Premiere ligne des Angloïs, en avant de la quelle sont des redoutes, et des Batteries entre chacunne,
le tout envelloppé par un Abbattis.
i Batterie de 11 pieces de Canon dont 9 pour deffendre le passage de Easton Beack.
k Fort Tominy Hill.
l Mamelon en avant de Tominy Hill, dont le Sommet est occuppé par une redoute, les revers par une
redans couvert d'un abbattis.
m Seconde ligne des Angloïs, avec quatre redoutes.
n Batteries pour deffendre l'Entrée du Port.
o flotte Commandée par M.r le Comte d'Estaing pour aller combattre celle du lord Howe, le 10.=
Aoust 1778 au mattin.
p Fregattes Stationnées dans la passe de l'Est, pour protéger le mouvement des Americains.
q ouvrages construits par les Americains le 10 pour couvrir le front de la 1.re position qu'ils ont =
occuppé après le débarquement.
r Seconde position occuppée le 19 par les Americains avec les ouvrages qui la couvre rr Redouttes Projettées.
s Batterie de 2 pieces de Canons faitte le 10 pour protéger une retraite.
t Approches et batteries des Americains contre les lignes des angloïs, les deux premieres ont commencées
à jouer le 19 et les autres Successivement, le feu n'a cessé que le 28 au soir que l'on a totalement =
évacuées ces Batteries.
u ligne Construite par les Americains après la retraite dans la partie du Nord de l'Isle, qui à été
faite la nuit du 28 au 29.
x Point ou devoient debarquer les trouppes françoises pour se joindre à l'Aile gauche, commandée
par le General la Fayette.
y lieu de la retraitte des americains la nuit du 30 au 31 aoust
z Position des ennemis lors de la retraite.
& flotte Commandée par lord Howe.

N.a que la Couleur jaune Indique l'Armée Americaine et les Ouvrages Construits
par eux et que celle rouge designe ceux des Angloïs. les mots, Ferry, passage
d'eau ou Bacq. et celui, Bridge, Pont.

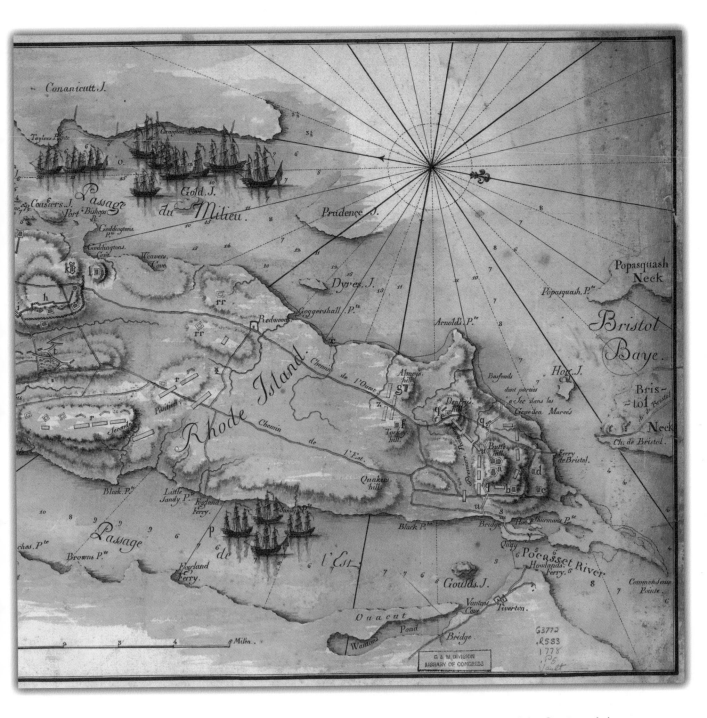

The map is a 1778 French map of Rhode Island showing the positions and operations of the Continental Army commanded by Major General John Sullivan (1740-1795) and the French fleet. It depicts their battles against the British Forces during the Battle of Rhode Island (Quaker Hill and the Siege of Newport) on 29 August 1778 until their eventual retreat on the night of 30 August 1778.

Top left: Admiral of the Fleet Richard Howe, 1726-1799, 1st Earl Howe (1726-1799). Portrait as an Admiral in undress uniform, 1787-1795 pattern, of a blue jacket with gold braid and his own white hair, by John Singleton Copely, National Maritime Museum, Greenwich London, Caird Collection.

Top right: Major-General Sir Robert Pigot, 2nd Baronet (1720-1796) Portrait as a Lieutenant-Colonel in the uniform of the 38th Regiment of Foot, ca. 1763, by Francis Coates, Parker Gallery, London.

Bottom left: General Sir Henry Clinton (1730-1795). British Commander in Chief during the American Revolution Portrait about 1762-1765. Attributed to Andrea Soldi, American Museum & Gardens, Bath.

The Battle of Rhode Island in 1778

THE OFFICIAL BRITISH VIEW AS REPORTED IN

The London Gazette

A FACSIMILE *with*
an INTRODUCTION *and*
an ANNOTATED TRANSCRIPTION

by JOHN B. HATTENDORF
D.Phil., D.Litt. (Oxon.)
Historian, Rhode Island Society Sons of the Revolution

Rhode Island Society Sons of the Revolution

2021

Published in 2021
By Stone Tower Press
For the Rhode Island Society Sons of the Revolution

Stone Tower Press
7 Ellen Rd.
Middletown, RI 02842
stonetowerpress.com

ISBN: 978-1-7368651-0-1

Formatting and cover design by Amy Cole, JPL Design Solutions

Printed in the United States of America

Table of Contents

Acknowledgements

At the Naval War College, the editor acknowledges with great appreciation the assistance of Mrs. Elena Bonilla for her assistance with the initial transcription. Members of the College's HHC Working Group—including Doug Chamberlain, Rob Dahlin, Tim Demy, Dave Kohnen, John Kuehn, Jamie McGrath, Craig Symonds, Geoff Till, and Evan Wilson—provided valuable constructive criticism to an early draft. In addition, Dr. John A. Houlding has generously provided biographical information on regular officers of the British Amy from his private database of *Georgian Military Officers*. Lieutenant Colonel Donald M. Londahl-Smidt (USAF, Ret.), the Director of Military Research at the Johannes Schwalm Historical Association, provided valuable information on the German Auxiliary Troops. Dr. Gina Palmer helpfully proofread several versions of the galley proofs. I am grateful for the additional assistance and advice of Professor Gregory Unwin of Temple University, Donald Hagist, and Dr. D. K. Abbass of the Rhode Island Marine Archaeology Project.

Sources of information for the Introduction are cited in the notes. The additional information in the annotated text on British officers was gathered from the Brian Harrison, et al, eds., *Oxford Dictionary of National Biography* (Oxford: Oxford University Press, 2007); David Syrett and R. L. Di Nardo, comps., *The Commissioned Sea Officers of the Royal Navy, 1660-1815.* Occasional Publication of the Navy Records Society, No. 1 (Aldershot: Scolar Press for the Navy Records Society, 1994); Nicholas Tracy, *Who's Who in Nelson's Navy* (London: Chatham, and St Paul, MN: MBI Publishing, 2006), and the websites *Three Decks—Warships in the Age of Sail* https://threedecks.org/ and *More than Nelson: The Royal Navy 1776-18115: A Biographical History and Chronicle* https://morethannelson.com/.

The information on Loyalists is from Walter T. Dornfest, comp., *Military Loyalist of the American Revolution: Officers and Regiments* (Jefferson, NC: McFarland & Co., 2011); Lorenzo Sabine, comp., *Biographical Sketches of Loyalists of the American Revolution* (Boston: Little Brown, 1864).

Information on German Auxiliary Troops has come from Walter K. Schroder, *The Hessian Occupation of Newport and Rhode Island, 1776-1779* (NP: Heritage Books, 2005) and from Lieutenant Colonel Donald M. Londahl-Smidt's, *German Troops in the American Revolution (1): Hessen- Cassel* (Oxford: Osprey, 2021).

Information on British warships has come from Rif Winfield, *British Warships in the Age of Sail, 1714-1792: Design, Construction, Careers and Fates* (Barnsley: Seaforth Publishing, 2007); D. K. Abbas, *Rhode Island in the Revolution: Big Happenings in the Smallest Colony.* Part II: *The Ships Lost in Rhode Island.* 2nd ed. (USDI National Park Service, American Battlefield Protection Program,

Grant # GA-2255-01-012, 2006); and Michael Crawford, Dennis Conrad, and Peter Luebke, eds., *Naval Documents of the American Revolution,* (Washington: Naval History and Heritage Command, 2019), vol. 13: *American and European Theaters, 1 June 1778 – August 15, 1778.* Information on French warships is from my own, *Newport, The French Navy, and the American Revolution* (Newport: The Redwood Press, 2005) and Rif Winfield and Stephen S. Roberts, *French Warships in the Age of Sail, 1626-1786: Design, Construction, Careers and Fates* (Barnsley: Seaforth, 2017).

J.B.H.
Newport, Rhode Island
January 2021

Introduction

Since the mid-1660s, *The London Gazette* has been the British government's official publication of record. First published on 16 November 1665 during King Charles II's reign, the *Gazette* appeared two years after the King had granted his charter to the English Colony of Rhode Island and Providence Plantations. It was first printed in Oxford, where the King and the court had taken temporary refuge while the plague ravaged London. Samuel Pepys noted in his diary on 22 November 1665, "This day the first of the *Oxford Gazettes* came out, which is very pretty, full of news, and no folly in it. . . ."[1] When King Charles and the Court returned to London on 1 February 1666, the *Gazette* changed its name and became known as *The London Gazette*, the name under which it still appears today.[2]

The London Gazette is Britain's oldest continuously operating newspaper, although, as a government publication, it has always been quite different than the free press. During the turmoil of the seventeenth-century Civil War and subsequent Restoration of the monarchy in England, the English government took the view that the open publication of news was a danger to national security.[3] With the lapse of the Licensing Act in 1695, the number of newspapers grew exponentially. By the time of the American Revolution, an estimated fourteen million copies were printed. At the same time, newspapers became intricately linked to political discourse and party rivalry.[4] *The Gazette* was a means by which the government attempted to control the press, but this was never wholly successful. In general, *The Gazette* successfully acted as the government's conduit to release otherwise highly restricted information on foreign, military, and naval affairs.

The King, represented by a Secretary of State, was the ultimate authority for the publication of the *Gazette*. Over the following century, the *Gazette*'s work centered on the offices of the secretaries of state. The Secretary of State created a staff position in 1665, "Writer of Gazette," and then in 1751 added a "Deputy Writer of Gazette," who reported to the Under Secretary of State. These appointments were

---

1   Robert Latham and William Matthews, eds., *The Diary of Samuel Pepys.* (London: G, Bell & Sons, 1972), volume VI - 1665, p. 305. Since the first issue appeared on 16 November 1665 in Oxford, Pepys probably saw the second issue, which appeared in Oxford and was then reprinted in London about 22 November.

2   P. M. Handover, *A History of the London Gazette, 1665-1965.* (London: Her Majesty's Stationery Office, 1965), pp. 11, 13.

3   On this subject, see J. Walker, "The Censorship of the Press during the Reign of Charles II," *History*, new series, vol. 35, no. 125 (October 1950), pp. 219-238; David Ogg, *England in the Reign of Charles II.* Second edition. (Oxford: Oxford University Press, 1956, reprinted in one volume, 1972), pp. 709-711.

4   Jeremy Black, "Newspapers and Politics in the Eighteenth Century," *History Today*, vol. 36, no. 10 (1986).

made for life and often became sinecures, with deputies doing the actual work. From 1714 to 1770, the Writer of Gazette received a salary of £300 per year. He, in turn, paid his deputy £30 a year.

These were notable perquisites for a civil servant when the average annual income for military and naval officers was £80 to £100; an ordinary merchant seaman, £20; and a common soldier £14.[5] In 1770, Lord Grafton, Secretary of State for the Northern Department, rewarded his Under Secretary of State, William Fraser, with a life appointment as Writer. Fraser held this position when this issue appeared and for another twenty-five years until 1803.[6] As the *Gazette*'s historian has written, "Fraser was a lieutenant, careful and punctual but content to leave initiative to others."[7]

For its contents, the *Gazette* was dependent upon reports sent from embassies to the secretaries of state and dispatches from military and naval commanders forwarded to the War Office and Admiralty. In 1769, Secretary of State Lord Weymouth reminded potential contributors that they should take "particular care, as the *Gazette* is the only paper of authority in this country, never to send anything concerning which there is any doubt."[8] During wartime in the eighteenth century, however, readers doubted the veracity of the reports they read, suspecting that bad news was being suppressed and exaggerating the good news. Several critics suspected Lord George Germain, Secretary of State for the Colonies from 1775 to 1782, of doing this.[9] Indeed, from time to time, the Admiralty, War Office, and Secretaries of State redacted the military and naval reports that they sent to the *Gazette* so as not to publish information that would assist the enemy, unnecessarily distress the families of soldiers and sailors, or unduly embarrass the government. In the case of the naval report by Captain Brisbane, printed here, there were no redactions. Research has not yet shown whether or not any information was omitted or changed in Major-General Pigot's dispatch.

Typically, local newspapers and journals reprinted or summarized the newsworthy and authoritative reports that had first appeared in the *London Gazette*. For example, the dispatch from Major-General Pigot also appeared, among other places, in the [London] *Public Advertiser* (29 October 1778), the

---

5 Peter H. Lindhert and Jeffrey G. Williamson, "Revising England's Social Tables 1688-1812," *Explorations in Economic History*, vol. 19 (1982), pp. 285-408, at pp. 395-396. The benchmark figures used here are for 1759.

6 J. C. Sainty, *Officials of the Secretaries of State, 1660-1782*. (London: Athlone Press for the Institute of Historical Research, 1973), pp. 44-45.

7 Handover, *A History of the London Gazette*, p. 58.

8 Circular from Lord Weymouth, 7 July 1769, Calendar of Home Office papers, 1766-1769, p. 483, quoted in Handover, *A History of the London Gazette*, p. 57.

9 Mark A. Thomson, *The Secretaries of State, 1681-1782*. (Oxford: Clarendon Press, 1932; reprinted London: Frank Cass, 1968), pp. 148-150.

Stamford Mercury (29 October 1778), the *Dublin Evening Post* (5 November 1778), and Dublin's *Saunders's News-Letter* (7 November 1778).[10]

Over the centuries, the *Gazette* has given rise to several nuanced expressions in the English language. From the mid-18th century, a person who was the subject of an official announcement in the *Gazette* for promotions, awards, or honors from the armed forces, diplomatic service, and other government service was said to have been "gazetted." Similarly, an officer whose resignation was announced in the *Gazette* was "gazetted out." Additionally, from the time of the Boer War in 1899-1902, when an official military or naval dispatch published in the *London Gazette* mentioned an individual for their actions, this became the distinction of being "mentioned in dispatches."[11]

The Rhode Island Campaign of 1778 in Strategic and Operational Perspective. During the War for American Independence, military and naval operations had been in progress for more than two years when the Rhode Island Campaign took place. The initial British strategy was two-pronged, designed to both crush the Army led by George Washington and to occupy the major port cities—Boston, New York, Philadelphia, and eventually, Charleston—where British leaders mistakenly thought the heart of the rebellion lay. In this, Newport and Narragansett Bay initially appeared to be advantageous for a fleet anchorage.

By 1778, the British military campaign had failed to make effective use of Britain's military and naval superiority against the rebels in North America. General Sir William Howe's tactical victories at Germantown, Brandywine, and Philadelphia had minimal strategic effect. The American victory at Saratoga in 1777, with the surrender of General Burgoyne's Army, served to build on a sense of moral superiority among Americans. This sense began at Bunker Hill in 1775 and continued through Trenton in 1776 and on to the final battle at Yorktown. The Battle of Saratoga in September 1777 provided the pretext for France to enter the war and begin to pressure Spain to join in a Franco-Spanish alliance against Britain.[12]

When France signed its treaty of alliance with the United States and the war between Britain and France began in February 1778, it killed the British Army's plan to reinforce General Sir Henry Clinton so that his Army could act offensively against the American rebels. Now Britain needed to counter France and use her troops in North America to defend her possessions in the West Indies. The

---

10 See the British Newspaper Archive. https://www.britishnewspaperarchive.co.uk/ . I am grateful to Dr. D. K. Abbass for providing a copy of the article in the *Public Advertiser*.

11 *Oxford English Dictionary* online. See "gazetted" and "mentioned in dispatches" under "mention."

12 Jonathan R. Dull, *The French Navy and American Independence: A Study of Arms and Diplomacy, 1774-1787* (Princeton: Princeton University Press, 1975), pp. 89-94.

rebellion in America was now a secondary issue. From the perspective of several ministers in the British government in early 1778, British finances and the British economy depended on British possession of the West Indies. If Britain fully controlled all the West Indian islands, this would give Britain the ability to control the North American colonies' economy, which was dependent on their West Indian trade. The thought of controlling the West Indies brought with it visions of profit and compensation for British losses in the war, a favorable balance of trade, and a tool to coerce the rebellious colonists. At the same time, it would also punish France by taking her Caribbean colonies that appeared to be the economic source for French military and naval power. In January 1778, King George III was considering the complete withdrawal of British forces from the North American colonies, retaining only Canada and Nova Scotia in the North with West and East Florida in the South. The ministry decided that the King would offer peace to the Americans, offering them a union with equal freedom under a common sovereign to govern themselves without reference to Britain, but acting together for their mutual safety.[13]

After an extensive debate, ministers decided that complete withdrawal from North America seemed overly risky. It would encourage the Americans to build up their Navy to attack the West Indies. While sending a squadron of four ships of the line, three 50-gun ships, and four frigates to the Leeward Islands, the Admiralty, at the same time, recalled twenty frigates and sloops from North America to fill the severe shortage of cruisers in home waters. The Admiralty and War Office also planned to move five thousand troops from Philadelphia in transports and use them to attack the island of St Lucia, while also planning to send another three thousand men to reinforce East and West Florida. After these detachments, the remnant of the Philadelphia garrison would withdraw to New York, and from there, make another detachment to reinforce Halifax, Nova Scotia.

The Peace Commissioners were sent immediately to America. If they found no success, or if the military or naval forces were in danger, Clinton was to evacuate New York. The execution of these plans would reduce the British military position in North America to holding the northern and southern flanks while occupying only two ports in rebel territory: New York City and Newport, Rhode Island. British officials silently abandoned their plans to develop a major British naval base in New York City. The Peace Commissioners planned to use the potential threat the naval base posed as a point of negotiation.[14]

In all these plans, British ministers based their strategy on the assumption that the Royal Navy retained full command of the Western Atlantic. Britain would be able to move her forces between North

---

13 Piers Mackesy, *The War for America, 1775-1783* (London: Longmans Green, & Co. 1964), pp. 220-221.

14 Mackesy, *War for America*, pp. 184-188.

America and the West Indies without interference. King Louis XVI and his ministers in France, still smarting from French naval defeats during the Seven Years' War, had some doubts about their military and naval capabilities against Britain. They saw two major strategic options: to force a battle in the Channel as a prelude to invading Britain or defeating British forces on a distant station by exploiting their local superiority. On reflection, Louis XVI and his ministers agreed on a compromise approach. They decided to threaten Britain with an invasion at home to the degree that the British government could not concentrate forces overseas while at the same time placing their priority on defending their possessions in the West Indies and assisting the American colonies.

Britain was not prepared for a major war in Europe. Her home military defenses were weak and vulnerable. Britain had already made a large military and naval commitment in America, while France had no existing obligations. The French Navy was in a more advanced state of readiness than the British fleet in European waters. Faced with this situation, Louis XVI's ministers, led by the Comte de Vergennes, saw that France had an opportunity during a limited period to make a decisive effect in an overseas theater. Britain was temporarily unable to defend herself at home deal with a significant threat abroad. The French Mediterranean squadron based at Toulon had been preparing for deployment for the past two years. Under the command of the Comte d'Estaing, the senior active-duty officer in the French Navy, it could be used for the distant theater, while the Brest Squadron could maintain the threat in British home waters.[15]

D'Estaing sailed from Toulon Roads on 13 April 1778 with twelve ships of the line and five frigates. The Admiralty in London received intelligence of d'Estaing's departure, but not of his destination. The Royal Navy had the opportunity to attack the French squadron at the Strait of Gibraltar but hesitated to do so without a clearer understanding of French objectives. The ministry in London did not want to initiate hostilities as they clearly understood their weakness at home. Admiral Augustus Keppel, commanding the fleet in the Channel, could not abandon home waters or weaken his fleet with detachments to attack d'Estaing's fleet located south of the French Navy's base at Brest squadron. The French wanted to delay hostilities so that d'Estaing could reach North American waters without incident and so that a replacement squadron could prepare for Mediterranean operations. Simultaneously, for the sake of appearances, the French ministry wanted to force Britain into being the aggressor.

In mid-May, the ministry in London was still trying to determine d'Estaing's destination but had taken the precaution of having a squadron of reinforcements under Vice-Admiral the Hon. John Byron

---

15 Mackesy, *War for America*, pp. 191-192; Dull, *The French Navy and American Independence*, pp. 105-112; John B. Hattendorf, *Newport, The French Navy and the American Revolution* (Newport: The Redwood Press, 2005), pp. 1-3.

begin preparations to sail. Finally receiving confirmation that d'Estaing was crossing the Atlantic on 2 June, the Admiralty ordered Byron to sail for New York on 7 June with thirteen ships of the line.

Three weeks later, on 28 June, Admiral Richard, Lord Howe, the Commander in Chief of the North American station, had just arrived off the Delaware Capes to evacuate the British Army from the Philadelphia area. As he arrived, he received the dispatches from London that advised him that d'Estaing was crossing the Atlantic to assist the Americans. Byron, with a similar-sized force, was in pursuit, heading for New York. The frigate carrying the dispatches had sighted d'Estaing's ships in the mid-Atlantic and reported that Howe should expect them within a week. At the same time, Byron was unlikely to arrive for several weeks at the earliest. With this intelligence, Admiral Howe and General Sir Henry Clinton, the senior British military commander in North America, could do little more than hurry along with their evacuation of Philadelphia and speed the concentration of their forces at New York while beginning to make contingency preparations to fight the French.

Moving with alacrity, the transports carrying the supplies for Clinton's Army reached Sandy Hook, New Jersey, and were all safely over the bar and in New York Bay on 1 July. On the same day, Clinton's dispatches arrived, reporting that he had fought an indecisive action with Washington's troops at Monmouth Court House on 28 June. He was now waiting at Navesink, near Sandy Hook, for transport ships to take his troops across New York Bay to their new assignments on Staten Island, Long Island, and Manhattan. Howe acted immediately and succeeded in evacuating the entire British force from New Jersey by 5 July. Still not knowing the French objective, Howe prepared fourteen of his largest ships for sea while he and Clinton planned for various contingencies. If the French attacked British positions at Halifax or Rhode Island, they prepared to relieve the British garrisons stationed in those places. However, if the French put in at an American port for repairs, water, and supplies, that might allow Howe and Clinton to continue with their still-pending plans to attack St Lucia in the West Indies, send an expedition to Florida, and still attack d'Estaing's squadron at a later point.[16]

On the evening of 7 July, after being at sea for three months, d'Estaing finally arrived off the Delaware Capes. Anchoring the next day, he ordered the frigate *Chimère* to take France's first ambassador to the United States, Conrad Alexandre Gérard de Rayneval, up the Delaware River to the American seat of government at Philadelphia. On the same day, a British frigate arrived at New York with the intelligence that she had sighted the French steering north off the coasts of Virginia and that the frigate *Mermaid* and the sloop *Haerlem* were trailing them. The following day, 8 July, *Haerlem* arrived in New York with confirmation that the French were off the mouth of the Delaware River. With

---

16 Ira D. Gruber, *The Howe Brothers and the American Revolution* (Chapel Hill: University of North Carolina Press for the Institute of Early American History and Culture at Williamsburg, 1972), pp. 304-306.

this information in hand, Howe and Clinton concluded that they must set aside the idea of attacking the West Indies and garrisoning the Floridas. They now assumed that d'Estaing would only look in at New York, before attacking Newport, Rhode Island, on his way to Boston for supplies and repairs.

Howe and Clinton worked together closely. They immediately sent 1,500 men on ships through Long Island Sound to strengthen the garrison at Newport. Then, Howe began to speed preparations of his ships. He quickly raised one thousand volunteers to take the places of the sailors, who were sick ashore. At the same time, he sent a dispatch to Vice-Admiral Byron to hurry his arrival on the southern New England coast. By 9 July, contrary winds had prevented Howe from bringing all his large ships down New York Bay to Sandy Hook. Eight major warships were still at Staten Island, where they had gone to get fresh water. It was not until the morning of 11 July that Clinton and Howe gave any serious thought to defending New York. Up to this point, they had assumed that the French would make for Newport, the weaker of the two British military garrisons and the easier place to reach.[17]

Meanwhile, after delivering the ambassador, d'Estaing moved north along the New Jersey coast to Sandy Hook, where he arrived on the afternoon of 11 July. Even with the news of the appearance off Sandy Hook, the British commanders seemed more concerned about the safety of the Rhode Island garrison and the reinforcements heading in that direction than in using their ships to attack the French off New York. Only after the French fleet had been at anchor for several days off Sandy Hook did they suddenly realize the need to improve Sandy Hook's defenses and those around New York Bay. Sandy Hook was particularly vulnerable. If the French captured the land defenses, Howe thought they could work their ships across the bar and destroy the smaller British fleet. As it was, however, the two anchored, opposing fleets just observed each other out of gun range with the British inside the bay and the French outside, separated by Sandy Hook and the sandbars, unable to find pilots to take them across the treacherous bar.[18]

British Army Captain John Pebbles of the 42nd Regiment of Foot, "the Black Watch," noted in his diary that the port of New York was "complatly block'ed up, and what I believe never was the case before a British Admiral block'd up in Harbour, by a French fleet."[19] The British tactical situation at New York was not unlike that of the French, who were typically the ones on the other foot, facing a British blockade of Brest, Toulon, and elsewhere. In this case, if the two opposing squadrons had been

---

17 Gruber, *The Howe Brothers*, pp. 305-306.

18 Hattendorf, *Newport, the French Navy, and the American Revolution*, pp. 9-10.

19 Ira D. Gruber, ed., *John Pebbles' American War, 1776-1782*. Publications of the Army Records Society, vol. 13 (Stroud, Gloucestershire: Sutton Publishing, 1998), p. 202.

facing one another in the open sea, d'Estaing's twelve ships of the line and six frigates clearly would have had an overwhelming advantage over Howe's six ships of the line and twelve frigates.

The situation at Sandy Hook involved the French having to attempt to cross a shallow bar and then navigate a narrow channel between the sandbanks one or two ships at a time. The largest French ships were deep draft, drawing between 22 to 27 feet of water. At low tide, the bar had only 17 or 18 feet of water over it, but it had up to 30 feet at high tide. Thus, there was only a short window of time each day when the tide was favorable. Howe had also placed several frigates near the bar to fire at the French if they attempted to cross it. If they were to get over the bar, Howe had anchored his six sixty-gun ships in a concave line stretching north from the tip of Sandy Hook to the northwest. The configuration of the line allowed each ship an unobstructed field of fire along the channel and across it, with the further ability for each ship to counter the wind and tide by maintaining the angle of her position using spring lines.[20]

Not knowing the actual naval strength of British naval forces at New York, d'Estaing assumed there were 14 ships of the line, "a throng of frigates and a multitude of transports." As he wrote George Washington, "This superiority of number and the goodness of the English navy will not hinder me from attacking Lord Howe in his retrenchment and under his batteries, if the depth of the water do not forbid me."[21] Lieutenant Colonel Alexander Hamilton was Washington's personal liaison to d'Estaing. With the intelligence of British naval reinforcements coming under Byron, the difficulties in engaging the British at New York, and the barrier that the depth of water provided, d'Estaing accepted the suggestion that Hamilton had brought with him from Washington to move on to Rhode Island. Waiting only for the return of the frigate *Chimère* from Philadelphia, d'Estaing sailed from the anchorage off Sandy Hook on 22 July.[22]

Howe was astonished by the French departure but took no immediate action. On the 25 July, Howe had intelligence that the French were buffeting headwinds and sailing in an easterly direction and unlikely to return to attack New York. Their objective was still not clear, but given their general direction and the winds, the options seemed to be Newport, Boston, or even the West Indies. With no information about Byron's whereabouts, Howe initially decided to wait at New York and postpone any

---

20 Gruber, *Howe Brothers*,

21 D'Estaing to Washington, 17 July 1778: David R. Hoth, ed., *The Papers of George Washington. Revolutionary War Series*, vol. 16, *July-September 1778.* (Charlottesville: University of Virginia Press, 2006), p. 90.

22 Gruber, *Howe Brothers*, pp. 308-310; Hamilton to Washington, 20 July 1778 and 23 July 1778, Hoth, ed., *Papers of George Washington*, pp. 109-110, 141-142.

action until reinforcements arrived. While Howe waited, an additional ship came from the West Indies, and two others were en route from Halifax, in addition to those he expected in Byron's squadron.

With further intelligence that indicated that the French were now on a northeasterly course for Rhode Island, Howe met with Clinton. The general advised him of current military intelligence that reported the Americans had been concentrating ground forces in Rhode Island for some time. This information stirred Clinton to act. By the end of July, he had enough ships to consider engaging d'Estaing. On 2 August, Clinton confirmed his decision to act with the news that d'Estaing had arrived off Newport on 30 July.

Nevertheless, contrary winds prevented Howe's departure from New York Bay until 6 August. General Clinton remained behind at New York, having agreed that it was "inexpedient" for them both to go. Clinton put great confidence in Major-General Pigot, who was commanding the Newport garrison. Clinton recalled, "I had the pleasure early in August to receive information from him '*that he had secured most of his provisions and ammunition, and that he did not know that anything was wanting,*' which put me perfectly easy with respect to his situation."[23] Howe took only enough of Clinton's troops with him to supply the deficiency in the Marines he usually carried on board. In the meantime, Clinton ordered 4,000 men under Major-General Sir Charles Grey to be ready for instant embarkment in transports at Flushing, New York.[24]

While Howe had made up his mind to support British forces against the French at Newport, he had no clear plan for doing so. Despite the naval reinforcements, he and his officers realized the risk of engaging the still numerically superior French forces. Privately, he confessed great reluctance to fight, hoping only to lure the French away from Rhode Island without a battle. Howe expected to find on his arrival that French troops had already landed and that the Newport garrison was in a dire position. However, at his appearance off Newport on 9 August, messengers from the shore reported a different situation: d'Estaing's squadron was just preparing to land its troops and join with the recently arrived American Continental soldiers and militia. The arrival of Howe's squadron offshore served to distract the French from their intentions. They immediately reembarked what troops and cannon they had put ashore, concerned that they could be blockaded in Narragansett Bay with hostile forces on the shores around them. On the day after Howe's arrival, d'Estaing led his squadron past the British batteries

---

23 William B. Willcox, ed. *The American Rebellion: Sir Henry Clinton's Narrative of his Campaigns, 1775-1782, with an Appendix of Documents* (New Haven: Yale University Press, 1954), p. 102. Clinton's italics.

24 Gruber, *Howe Brothers*, pp. 309-311; Clinton, *The American Rebellion*, p. 102.

and out to sea to face Howe in standard fleet battle formation, only to have the opposing warships dispersed under high winds and heavy seas that approached hurricane conditions.[25]

On the day that the French squadron put to sea, Major General John Sullivan crossed over from Tiverton to the northern end of Aquidneck Island with the Continental Army troops and militia under his command. The American forces advanced from Portsmouth through Middletown toward Newport, where they took up positions along the British lines defending Newport. As the Americans opened their batteries, d'Estaing's storm-battered squadron returned and anchored off Newport on 20 August but was in no condition to provide substantial support. Aware that Admiral Byron's squadron of reinforcements was approaching the area, d'Estaing decided to stay 24 hours at anchor off Newport before sailing on to Boston. The prevailing southwest wind helped the French round Cape Cod and Georges Bank to reach Boston, while it held Byron back, forcing him to go into Halifax, Nova Scotia, instead of New York or Newport.

At this point, apparently, neither Howe nor Clinton had thought about the option of supporting one another directly at Newport. Then en route to Newport from New York after the storm, Howe heard the news of the French departure on 25 August. He immediately decided to intercept d'Estaing at sea to prevent him from reaching Boston. Taking the shorter, more dangerous route between Nantucket Shoals and Georges Bank, Howe failed in his attempt, losing a ship aground on Cape Cod and reaching Boston two days after the French had put into port.[26]

On 27 August, Sir Charles Grey was embarking his 4,000 troops at Flushing, New York, when Clinton received a similar report from Pigot that the French had left Narragansett Bay and the coast of southern New England, but that the American forces remained in position. With that intelligence, Clinton decided to sail immediately through Long Island Sound to Rhode Island, with Grey and his troops, to raise the Americans' siege of the Newport garrison and take advantage of whatever opportunities arose. Calm and, then contrary, winds slowed their passage from Flushing.

The delay gave time for General Sullivan to withdraw American forces from Aquidneck Island. Meanwhile, the events described in this issue of the *London Gazette* had taken place. Clinton had sent his adjutant-general, the 23-year-old Colonel Lord Rawdon, to Newport to explain to Pigot his plan to intercept the American retreat from Aquidneck Island. Clinton had planned on "runing up the Narragansett Passage to the Bristol Neck, where I proposed to land and seize their batteries, boats,

---

25 Clinton, *The American Rebellion*, p. 102.

26 Gruber, *Howe Brothers*, pp. 314, 318-319; Clinton, *The American Rebellion*, p. 102; Hattendorf, *Newport, the French Navy, and the American Revolution*, pp. 26-27.

stores &c."[27] Then, with frigates and galleys in the East Passage and Pigot's forces in the rear, Clinton thought he would have trapped Sullivan on the island. But this was not to be. Clinton arrived in Narragansett Bay the day after Sullivan had evacuated his troops from Aquidneck Island to Tiverton on 30 August. Disappointed, Clinton returned to New York, instructing Grey to attack American positions at New London and New Bedford.[28]

Clinton had already begun thinking about making an amphibious assault on the French forces at Boston; Howe disagreed with Clinton and thought that such an operation would be useless.[29] Both men soon returned to New York. Byron had not yet arrived at New York from Halifax but reported on 27 August that he was trying to come as quickly as possible. Lord Howe, anxious to return home before a new phase in the campaign began, resigned his duties as commander-in-chief of the North American Station on 8 September to his second in command, Rear-Admiral James Gambier, pending the arrival of Vice-Admiral Byron. Howe's resignation created a controversy in naval circles, where many thought Gambier an incompetent and "penurious old reptile."[30] Howe was still in America when Byron finally arrived. The two men met on 25 September at Newport, the day before Howe sailed for England. Howe urged Byron to go New York as soon as possible to relieve Gambier, make plans with Clinton, and have discussions with the Peace Commissioners. They were still hoping to persuade Congress to forgo independence.[31] These actions ended the British campaign in the northern theater in 1778.

Clinton, who had been gloomy about the military situation in North America both before and during the Rhode Island campaign, recovered some optimism. As soon as Gambier could organize troopships, Clinton sent the long-planned expeditions to the West Indies and Florida, but instead of abandoning New York, he retained some 14,000 men. D'Estaing's threat to New York had underscored to Clinton and the ministry at home the vulnerability of his Army's supplies and the lack of strategic flexibility. Simultaneously, the Rhode Island campaign revealed that the Royal Navy could not

---

27 Clinton, *The American Rebellion*, p. 103.

28 Clinton, *The American Rebellion*, pp. 103-104.

29 David Syrett, *Admiral Lord Howe: A Biography* (Annapolis: Naval Institute Press, 2006), pp. 85-87.

30 David Syrett, "'This penurious old reptile': Rear-Admiral James Gambier and the American War," *Historical Research*. vol. 74, no. 183 (February 2001), pp. 63–76.

31 Gruber, *Howe Brothers*, pp. 323-324.

defend the Newport garrison from a determined assault by a superior French force. This conclusion led to Clinton abandoning the Newport position in 1779.[32]

For the French, d'Estaing's 1778 campaign was a disappointment. In five months, d'Estaing had succeeded in taking or destroying only five British frigates and four corvettes. The British lost most of those at Newport by their own hand to prevent capture. D'Estaing, who left Boston for the West Indies in early November, just missed capturing en route the weakly defended expedition to St Lucia. After the British landed on the island, additional British naval forces efficiently defeated the French naval threat and repulsed a French landing. In January, Byron arrived in the West Indies with ten ships of the line, joining eight more from Britain to establish British naval supremacy in the Caribbean. D'Estaing had succeeded only in capturing Dominica and in preserving his own force.[33]

The Transcription. The transcriptions that follow are selections from the 24-27 October 1778 issue of the *London Gazette* that report the events relating to the Battle of Rhode Island. It is not a full transcription of the entire issue reproduced in facsimile from the copy available on the internet at the *London Gazette* website.[34] At the end of Captain Brisbane's dispatch dated 27 July, the editor of the *Gazette* has added in an italicized note, marked by three asterisks, that says, *"There being no Possibility of Printing the Whole of Lord Howe's Dispatches To-night, the Remainder will be published in a Supplemental Gazette To-morrow."* No such supplemental issue of the *Gazette* is found on the official website, nor is there a continuation of Howe's dispatch in a later issue.

The transcribed text preserves the original capitalization, spelling, and punctuation of the original printed version. The editor has italicized all ships' names for clarity and uniformity.

The Annotation. Throughout the excerpted sections from *The London Gazette*, the editor has used footnotes at the bottom of the page to clarify and to explain references in the text that might not readily be understood by the general reader. The editor has provided brief biographical sketches of each of the military and naval officers mentioned in the text. This aspect offers the reader information about a range of individuals who fought both ashore and afloat in Rhode Island to retain Rhode Island within the British Empire.

The London Gazette rarely mentioned ordinary British soldiers and sailors, except in terms of aggregate numbers of the size of units or numbers of casualties. Recent authors have provided highly readable and useful insights that offer a broad general understanding of the common men and the

---

32 Mackesy, *War for America*, pp. 222, 276.

33 Dull, *The French Navy*, pp. 123-124.

34 The website of the *London Gazette*: The Gazette | Official Public Record: www.thegazette.co.uk.

conditions in which they lived and worked.[35] Typically, the dispatches published in *The Gazette* limited their mention of individuals to officers at some level of command, those who had distinguished themselves by their actions, or those who were casualties. However, these documents include a list of the commanding officers of British warships involved in the 1778 Rhode Island campaign that widen that scope. The biographies in the footnotes about people mentioned in the text provide insight into the officers' backgrounds and careers. Many of the army officers and some of the naval officers were younger sons of aristocrats—some obtained peerages themselves either by inheritance or by distinguishing themselves in their professions. Although the available sources on officers' careers provide different approaches, readers will note similarities and differences in practices between the two services. Army officers could purchase their commissions, while the key to a naval officer's career was passing the examination for Lieutenant. Both services promoted retired officers by seniority after they had retired from active service. While the Navy was more of a meritocracy than the Army, both involved a degree of patronage based on religious, geographic, and political connections.[36]

Beyond the broad aspects of British military and naval officer social history, the notes also identify some interesting individuals who readers may not have known had participated in the Revolutionary War in Rhode Island. Among them, one might note Hyde Parker, who was Nelson's senior at the attack on Copenhagen in 1801; Edward Edwards, who brought home some of the *Bounty* mutineers in *Pandora* in 1791, and the evangelical officer, Commander James Gambier, who after his retirement as an admiral was instrumental in founding Kenyon College in Gambier, Ohio.

---

35 See, for example, Don H. Hagist, *Noble Volunteers: The British Soldiers Who fought the American Revolution* (Yardley, PA: Westholme Publishing, 2020) and Stephen Taylor, *Sons of the Waves: The Common Seaman in the Heroic Age of Sail* (New Haven: Yale University Press, 2020).

36 For further information on British military and naval careers in the eighteenth century, see Evan Wilson, *A Social History of British Naval Officers, 1775-1815* (Woodbridge: Boydell, 2017), J. A. Houlding, *Fit for Service: The Graining of the British Army, 1715-1795* (Oxford: Clarendon Press, 1981), and Alan J. Guy, *Oeconomy and Discipline: Officership and Administration in the British Army 1714-1763* (Manchester: Manchester University Press, 1985).

The London Gazette

Numb. 11921.

Published by Authority

From Saturday, October 24 to Tuesday, October 27, 1778

Whitehall, October 27, 1778.

The Dispatches, of which the following are Extracts, from General Sir Henry Clinton,[37] Knight of the Bath, to the Right Honourable Lord George Germain,[38] One of His Majesty's Principal Secretaries of State, were received on Sunday last, from Lieutenant Grove,[39] of His Majesty's Ship the *Apollo*,[40] which left New York on the 17th of September, and arrived at Plymouth on the 23d Instant.

---

37 **General Sir Henry Clinton** (1730-1795) succeeded General Sir William Howe as Commander in Chief, North America, in 1777 and served in that post until 1782.

38 **Lord George Germain**, later 1st Viscount Sackville, (1716-1785), was Secretary of State for the Colonies between 10 November 1775 and 10 February 1782. See Alan Valentine, *Lord George Germain* (Oxford: Clarendon Press, 1962).

39 **Thomas Saunders Grove** was born about 1737 and joined the Royal Navy on 18 July 1747. Grove passed his examination for Lieutenant on 6 September 1758, commissioned a Lieutenant in the Royal Navy on 21 November 1762. As a Lieutenant he commanded the 18-gun *Pondicherry* from 12 December 1780 to 2 March 1784, during which time he participated in the second Battle of Cuddalore on 20 June 1783. Promoted to Commander on 25 September 1809, he died in January 1814.

40 The 32-gun frigate ***Apollo,*** commanded by Captain Philemon Pownoll.

New York, September 15, 1778.

I had the Honour of receiving your Lordship's Dispatches of the 12 of June and 1st of July, by the *Lord Hyde* Pacquet,[41] on the 18th of that Month, and a Triplicate of your Letter No 7, by the *Lioness*,[42] on the 7th Instant.

I detached Major-General Tryon,[43] some Time ago, to the East End of Long Island, to secure the Cattle on that Part; in which situation he could either reinforce Rhode Island, or make a Descent on Connecticut, as Circumstances might occur; and Transports for 4,000 Men were laying then in the Sound, and that Number of Troops ready for Embarkation on the shortest Notice.

In this State Things were, when Lord Howe[44] sailed for Rhode Island; and it was my Intention to proceed up the Sound, with the Troops above-mentioned, that they might be within his Lordship's Reach, in case we should see an Opportunity for landing them to act with Advantage; but on the 27th of last Month, at the Instant they were embarked, I received a Letter from Lord Howe, inclosing one

---

41 The packet ship **Lord Hyde** is not listed in *Lloyd's Register of British and Foreign Shipping* for 1778.

42 The 26-gun armed storeship **Lioness** was a former East Indiaman, commanded by Commander William Grant in 1777-1779.

43 **William Tryon** was born in England on 8 June 1729 at the family home, Norbury Park, Surrey. He was a grandson of Robert Shirley, Earl Ferrers. Tryon became a Coronet in the Duke of Cumberland's 15th Dragoons in Flanders (or shortly to arrive there) on 27 February 1747/48, probably by purchase, vice a retirement. He went onto the British Half Pay List when the regiment disbanded on 3 February 1748/499. He transferred from Half Pay to be a Coronet in the 10th Dragoons in England on 22 May 1749. Tryon was promoted to Lieutenant and Captain in the 1st Foot Guards on 12 October 1751, by purchase. During the Seven Years War, he was involved in amphibious operations at Cherbourg and St Malo. During the withdrawal from the failed landing at St Cast, Tryon was wounded. He was promoted to the regimental rank of Captain-Lieutenant and Lieutenant-Colonel in the 1st Foot Guards on 30 September 1758, by purchase. Thereafter, he received his Army promotion to Captain and Lieutenant-Colonel on 9 December 1758, by purchase. Through family connections, he was appointed Lieutenant-Governor of North Carolina in 1764, and then became the Governor in 1765. He remained Governor in North Carolina until 1771, when he was appointed Governor of New York, a position he held until March 1780. While governor, he was given a commission as Brevet Colonel on 25 May 1772. He then purchased a commission as 3rd Major in the 1st Foot Guards on 8 August 1775. On 1 January 1776, he became Major-General with a local commission in America). He purchased a commission as 2nd Major in the 1st Foot Guards on 19 February 1776. He was promoted to Major-General in the British Army on 29 August 1777. On 14 May 1778, he became Colonel of the 70th Foot. He was promoted to Lieutenant-General on 20 November 1782. He became Colonel of the 29th Foot on 16 August 1783 and died on 27 January 1788 "at his house in Upper Grosvenor-str." after 39.6 years' service.

44 **Admiral Richard Howe, 4th Viscount Howe**, later 1st Baron Howe and 1st Earl Howe, (1726-1799), Commander in Chief, North American Station, 1776-1778.

from Major-General Pigot,[45] by which I was informed, that the French Fleet had quitted Rhode Island; but that the Rebels were still there in great Force.

I thought it adviseable to sail immediately for the Relief of that Place, but contrary Winds detained us till the 31st; and, on our Arrival, we found that the Enemy had evacuated the Island. For Particulars I must beg Leave to refer your Lordship to Sir Robert Pigot's Letter, a Copy of which I have the Honour to inclose. I was not without Hopes, that I should have been able to effect a Landing, in such Manner as to have made the Retreat of the Rebels from Rhode Island very precarious; or that an Opening would have offered for attacking Providence with Advantage: Being thwarted in both these Views by the Retreat of the Rebels, as the Wind was fair I proceeded towards New London, where I had Reason to believe there were many Privateers; but the Wind coming unfavourable just as I arrived

---

45 **Major-General Sir Robert Pigot**, second Baronet, was born on 20 September 1720. He was the second surviving son of Richard Pigot (1679-1729) and his wife Frances, a servant of Caroline, Princess of Wales. The Pigot family was of Huguenot descent. General Pigot was the brother of Sir George Pigot and Admiral Hugh Pigot. Robert Pigot was commissioned an Ensign in the 31st Regiment of Foot in 1741 and served with his regiment in the War of the Austrian Succession in Flanders. He was promoted to Lieutenant in 1744 and was present at the Battle of Fontenoy on 11 May 1745. In September 1745, he returned to England, then in 1749 served with his regiment in Minorca and then, Scotland. He was promoted to captain on 31 October 1751. In 1758, the 70th Regiment of Foot absorbed his battalion of the 31st Foot and on 5 May 1758, Pigot was promoted to Major. He joined the 38th Foot and advanced to Lieutenant-Colonel on 1 October 1764. He married Anne Johnson of Kilternan, Co. Dublin, in Ireland on 18 February 1765, with whom he had four children. In 1768, Robert succeeded his elder brother George as Member of Parliament for the venal and expensive constituency of Wallingford in Berkshire. He held the position until January 1772, when he was appointed Warden of the Mint. As a parliamentarian, he gave no known speeches, but voted for the Government on the Wilkes and Middlesex election issues in 1769. His attempt to stand for re-election to Parliament failed in 1772 and, at Stafford, in 1774. Promoted to Colonel in 1772, he and his regiment were ordered in 1774 from Ireland to North America, where the regiment was posted to Boston to quell the local disturbances. On 19 April 1775, he joined the relief force under Brigadier Hugh, Earl Percy, to support Lieutenant-Colonel Francis Smith's withdrawal from Lexington and Concord. Pigot distinguished himself at the Battle of Bunker Hill in June 1775, when he commanded the army's left wing with the local rank of Brigadier-General in the attack on the American redoubt on Charleston Heights. In a series of assaults, Pigot broke American resistance at great cost to his own men. To honor his bravery and distinguished service, King George III promoted him to colonel of the 38th Foot. He went with his regiment to Halifax, when the British Army evacuated Boston, then went to New York, where he commanded the second brigade at the Battle of Long Island on 27 August 1776. While still in America on 11 May 1777, Pigot succeeded on the death of his elder brother, George, to his baronetcy, inheriting at the same time his brother's estate at Patshull, Staffordshire, and a third of the £30,000 Pigot diamond. On 15 July 1777, Pigot took command of the British garrison at Newport and on 29 August 1777 was promoted to Major-General. In March 1778, he was under consideration to be named Howe's second in command, but this did not materialize. While in Rhode Island, the *bon vivant* Pigot was generally unhappy as he missed the social life in New York. Pigot relinquished his command in October 1779 and returned to England but saw no further active service. He was promoted to Lieutenant-General on 20 November 1782. After a long illness, he died at Patshull on 2 August 1796.

off that Port, and continuing so for Twenty-four Hours, I left the Fleet, directing Major-General Grey[46] to proceed to Bedford,[47] a noted Rendezvous for Privateers, &c. and in which there were a Number of captured Ships at that Time. For the Particulars of his Success, which has certainly been very complete, I must beg Leave to refer your Lordship to the inclosed Letter.

I am, &c.

H. CLINTON.

---

46 **Sir Charles Grey**, later 1st Baron Gray in 1801 and Earl Grey and Viscount Howick in 1806. He was born in Howick, Northumberland, about 23 October 1729, the son of Sir Henry Grey, 1st Baronet. He was commissioned an Ensign in the 6th Regiment of Foot in England on 18 December 1746, a free death vacancy, and served at Gibraltar. He was promoted to Lieutenant in the 6th Foot on 23 December 1752, by purchase vice a retirement. He became Captain of his own new-raising 46th Company, of Marines on 21 March 1755, then transferred to be Captain of the 20th Foot in England on 31 May 1755, serving under Lieutenant-Colonel James Wolfe. Serving with Wolfe, he participated in the unsuccessful attack on Rochefort in 1757. He was promoted to Lieutenant-Colonel Commandant in England of his own new-raising 98th Regiment of Foot on 27 January 1761, a free augmentation vacancy. During the Seven Years' War he served as adjutant on the staff of Prince Ferdinand of Brunswick-Lüneberg, who commanded the Hanoverian Army of Observation. He was wounded at Minden in 1759, commanded a company at the Battle of Kloster Kampen in 1760, was present at the capture of Belle-Isle in 1761 and at Havana in 1762, then served on the staff of Wilhelm, Graf zu Schaumburg-Lippe-Bückeburg, during the Spanish invasion of Portugal. He went onto the British Half Pay List when his regiment disbanded on 14 November 1763. He was promoted to Brevet Colonel on 20 December 1772 as ADC to HM King George III. From Half Pay, he became Colonel of the 28th Foot on 4 March 1777. During the War for American Independence, he was promoted to Major-General in America on 4 March 1777, then to Major-General in the British Army on 29 August 1777; he commanded the 3rd Brigade at the Battle of Brandywine in September 1777, at Germantown in October 1777, and Monmouth I June 1778. He was promoted to Lieutenant-General on 20 November 1782, then became Colonel of the 8th Light Dragoons on 13 July 1787; Colonel of the 7th Dragoon Guards on 17 March 1789. He was promoted to General on 26 September 1793 and commanded the West Indian Expedition to Martinique and Guadeloupe, He became Colonel of the 20th Light Dragoons on 4 November 1795. He served as Governor of Guernsey in the Channel Islands from 1797 to 1807. He was reappointed Colonel of the 8th Light Dragoons, 23 March 1797 and then Colonel of the 3rd Dragoons from 4 September 1799 until his death on 14 November 1807, after 47.6 years' service.

47 New Bedford, Massachusetts.

Copy of a Letter from Major-General Pigot to General Sir Henry Clinton, dated Newport, Rhode Island, August 31, 1778.

Though by my several Letters since the 29th of July last, more specially by that I had the Honour of writing by Lieutenant-Colonel Stuart,[48] and the Accuracy of his Intelligence, your Excellency will have been informed of the State of Affairs here to the 28th Instant; yet, as many of those Letters, from the Uncertainty of the Communication, may not have reached you, a Summary of the Transactions since the 29th of July, when the French Fleet[49] arrived, to the last Period, will not be unnecessary, and may help to explain subsequent Events.

From the start Appearance of the Fleet to the 8th Instant, our utmost Exertions were directed to removing to Places of Security the Provisions, Ammunition, and Military and Naval Stores, which were either on board Ship, or on the Wharfs, preparing a fortified Camp, and disposing every Thing for resisting the combined Attacks of the French and Rebels upon us; and I immediately withdrew from Conanicut Brown's Provincial Corps,[50] and two Regiments of Anspach,[51] which had been stationed there. The next Morning the Guns on the Beaver Tail and Dumplin Batteries, the former of which was

---

48 **Hon. Sir Charles Stuart.** Born in January 1753 at Kenwood House, Hampstead, England, he was the fourth and favorite son of John Stuart, 3rd Earl of Bute, and Mary Wortley Montagu. His father was a favorite of King George III and served as Prime Minister of Great Britain in 1762-63. When he was about to turn 16, Charles was commissioned an Ensign in the 37th Foot at Minorca on 23 November 1768, a free death-vacancy. He was promoted to Lieutenant in the 7th Foot in England, on 13 September 1770, by purchase vice a retirement. He was then promoted to Captain in the 35th Foot in England on 12 March 1773, by purchase vice a retirement. On 8 October, he was promoted, probably by purchase, to Major, commanding a battalion of the 43rd Foot in New England. probably by purchase. At New York City on 26 October 1777, he was promoted to Lieutenant-Colonel in the 26th Foot, by purchase, commanding the regiment until 1779. In 1776, he became Member of Parliament for the "rotten borough" of Bossiney in Cornwall. During a visit home to England in April 1778, he married Anne Louisa Bertie, daughter of the British politician Lord Vere Bertie. He returned to America, but remained only briefly before returning to England to become an Army liaison officer to the ministry and a critic of the British Army's conduct in America, although he remained a favorite of General Clinton's. Stuart was made Brevet Colonel on 20 November 1782. He transferred to Lieutenant-Colonel of the 101st Foot in the East Indies on 29 July 1784 and went onto the British Half Pay List when the regiment disbanded on 24 December 1785. He was promoted to Major-General on 12 October 1793. From Half Pay, he became Colonel of the 68th Foot on 24 October 1794, then Colonel of the 26th Foot on 25 March 1795. He was promoted to Lieutenant-General on 1 January 1798. He was briefly Governor of Minorca from 18 July 1799 and appointed Knight of the Bath in 1799. He died on 25 May 1801 at Richmond, Surrey, after 23.7 years' service.

49 **The 17-ship French fleet** was commanded by the Comte d'Estaing and consisted of two 80-guns ships of the line, six 74s, three 64s, one 50, and five 26-gun frigates.

50 **Captain David Brown** was a merchant from Boston who commanded a corps of loyal militia in 1778. Their service seems to have been entirely on Conanicut Island and, after their withdrawal, in defending Newport. After the war, Brown and his family went from New York to Shelburne, Nova Scotia, where the Crown granted him a lot of land in the town. He reported a loss of £300 for his loyalty.

51 **The troops of Margrave Friedrich Carl Alexander of Anspach-Bayreuth** were the Anspach regiment (commanded by Colonel Fredrich August Valentine Voit von Salzburg) and the Bayreuth Regiment (commanded by Colonel Johann Heinrich Wilhelm von Seybothen).

directed with some Effect against two Line of Battle Ships that entered the Narraganzet Passage, were rendered unserviceable, as the Fleet entering the Harbour would cut off all Communication with that Island; of which the French Admiral soon after took a temporary Possession, and landed the Marines of his Squadron. During this Period, from the Movements of the French Ships in the Seaconet on the 30th, the *King's Fisher*[52] and two Gallies[53] were obliged to be set on Fire; and afterwards, on the 5th Instant, the four advanced Frigates,[54] from the Approach of two of the Enemy's Line of Battle Ships from the Narraganzet, were likewise destroyed, after saving some of their Stores and securing the Landing of the Seamen.

When it was evident the French Fleet were coming into the Harbour, it became necessary to collect our Forces, and withdraw the Troops from the North Parts of the Island, which was accordingly done that Evening. I likewise ordered all the Cattle on the Island to be drove within our Lines, leaving only one Cow with each Family, and every Carriage and Intrenching Tool to be secured, as the only Measures that could be devised to distress the Rebels and impede their Progress.

On the 8th Instant, at Noon, the French Fleet (which from its first Appearance had continued with little Variation at Anchor about Three Miles from the Mouth of the Harbour) got under Way, and standing in under a light Sail, kept up a warm Fire on Brenton's Point, Goat Island, and the North Batteries, which were manned by Seamen of the destroyed Frigates, and commanded by Captain

---

52 The 14-gun, Swan Class ship sloop **Kingfisher** had been built at Chatham dockyard in 1769-70 to the 1766 design of John William. She had a gundeck length of 96 feet, 8 ½inches; keel length 78 feet 10 ½ inches; breadth 26 feet 10 inches; 302 8/94 tons BM. She was deliberately set on fire, broke from her anchorage, and eventually blew up off High Hill Point, Tiverton, Rhode Island, to avoid capture on 30 July 1778. Her remains have not yet been located. Their dimensions are unknown. *Spitfire* had 8 guns and carried 40 men.

53 **The galleys, *Alarm* and *Spitfire*** were sunk on 30 July 1778. *Alarm*, commanded by Lieutenant Philp Auvergne, was set afire and exploded south of McCorrie Point in the Sakonnet River, while *Spitfire*, commanded by Lieutenant James Saumarez, was set on fire and blew up, probably off High Hill Point, Tiverton. Their remains have not been located.

54 **The vessels purposely sunk** on 5 August 1778 were (1) the 32-gun Richmond Class frigate *Juno*, commanded by Captain Hugh Dalrymple, sunk in Coddington Cove whose remains have not been found but might possibly be the structure found off the east side of Coddington Point in Newport; (2) the 32-gun, modified Lowestoffe Class frigate *Orpheus*, commanded by Captain Charles Hudson, sunk off Melville; (3), the 28-gun, Coventry Class frigate *Cerberus*, commanded by Captain John Symons, sunk about 400 feet off shore south of Carr Point, Middletown; (4) the 32-gun, modified Richmond Class frigate *Lark*, commanded by Captain Richard Smith, sunk off the south side of Arnold's Point in Portsmouth.

Christian,[55] Lieutenants Forest[56] and Otway[57] of the Navy, who returned the Fire with great Spirit, and in a good Direction. The last of these Works had been previously strengthened, and some Transports sunk in its Front, as an effectual Measure to block up the Passage between it and Rose Island.

The next Morning we had the Pleasure to see the English Fleet, and I immediately sent on Board to communicate to Lord Howe our Situation, and that of the Enemy. By Nine o'Clock the following Day the French Fleet repassed our Batteries, and sailed out of the Harbour, firing on them as before, and having it returned with equal Spirit on our side. By this Cannonade from the Ships on both Days, very fortunately not One Man was hurt, or any Injury done, except to some Houses in Town.

I shall now proceed to inform your Excellency of the Movements of the Enemy from the 9th Instant, when they landed at Howland's Ferry.

---

55 **Hugh Cloberry Christian** was born in 1747, the only son of Lieutenant Thomas Christian (d. 1749) of Hook Norton, Oxfordshire, who had made a fortune as a privateer captain after leaving naval service. Hugh joined the Navy in 1761 and served in the Channel and the Mediterranean before he passed his Lieutenant's Examination in 1757. He was commissioned a Lieutenant in the Royal Navy on 21 January 1771. In 1776, he commanded a sloop *Shark* in the Leeward Islands. For his service in successfully escorting a convoy of merchant ships to New York with military supplies, he was assigned to the 64-gun *Eagle*, Admiral Lord Howe's flagship. Promoted to Commander on 24 January 1778, he took command of *Kingfisher*, which he destroyed on 30 July to prevent capture. Returning to England, he was promoted to Captain on 8 December 1778 and posted to command of the 74-gun *Suffolk*. Flying the broad pennant of Commodore, then the flag of Rear-Admiral Joshua Rowley, he returned to the Leeward Islands, where he participated in the Battle of Grenada on 6 July 1779, in which the ship had seven killed and twenty-five wounded. In November 1780, he took command of the recently captured 38-gun *Fortunée*. He participated in the Battle of the Chesapeake Capes in 1781, the Battle of St Kitts and the Battle of the Saintes in 1782. Returning him in 1783, he saw no service until ordered to command the new 74-gun *Colossus* from 1787 to 1790. He served briefly as Flag-Captain in command of the 100-gun *Princess Charlotte*, Lord Howe's flagship in the Channel, in October 1793, then again in February 1793 to April 1793. Thereafter he served as commissioner for French prizes after the Battle of the Glorious First of June, then Chairman of the Transport Board, 1794-95. Promoted to Rear-Admiral and soon after made a Knight Commander of the Order of the Bath, he served as Commander in Chief, Leeward Islands, commanding at the capture of St Lucia, St. Vincent, and Grenada in 1796. He returned to England and was named second in command at the Cape of Good Hope, then succeeded the command in May 1798. He was raised to the peerage as Lord Ronaldsway, but died at Cape Town on 21 November 1798, before the patent reached him. He was a distant relation of both Fletcher Christian and Brabazon Christian.

56 **Thomas Forrest** was commissioned a Lieutenant in the Royal Navy on 27 September 1775. He was first lieutenant in the frigate *Cerberus* and later killed in action on 16 January 1780.

57 **William Albany Otway** was born 26 July 1755 in London. He entered the Navy in 1764 and was commissioned a Lieutenant on 25 August 1773. While serving as second Lieutenant in the frigate *Lark* he was captured by the Americans while he was ashore hunting on the Potomac River in Virginia in August 1777. He was returned to his ship by the end of September and resumed his duties until his ship was purposely sunk to escape capture. After the Rhode Island operation, he was promoted to Commander on 28 March 1781, and to Captain on 1 December 1781. In 1795, he became a Commissioner of the Transport Board and served as Commissioner of the Gibraltar dockyard in 1803-04. He was promoted to Rear-Admiral on 2 October 1807. He was second in command under Rear-Admiral Sir Richard Strachan at the Walcheren operation in July 1809. He later served as commander in chief in the Thames and at Leith, eventually reaching the rank of Vice-Admiral before his death in 1815.

The Badness of the Weather for some Days must have prevented their transporting of Stores, or being in Read ness to approach us, as they did not make their Appearance near us 'till the 14th, when a large Body took Possession of Honyman's Hill.

To repel any Attempts from that Quarter, a Breastwork was directed to be made along the Heights from Green End to Irish Redoubt, which was strengthened by an Abbatis.[58]

On the 17th, the Enemy was discovered breaking Ground on Honyman's Hill, on the Summit of which, and on their Right of the Green End Road, they were constructing a Battery: The next Day another was commenced by them for Five Guns to their Left, and in a direct Line with the former, which was prepared for Four. On this Day a Line of Approach was likewise begun by them from the Battery on the Right to Green End Road, which Works we endeavoured to obstruct by keeping a continual Fire on them. The 19th the Enemy opened their Left Battery, which obliged our Encampment to be removed further in the Rear. This Day we began another Line, for the greater Security of our Left, from Irish's Redoubt to Fomini Hill;[59] and I directed a Battery of 1 Twenty four and 2 Eighteen Pounders to be raised on our Right Breast Work to counteract those of the Enemy, which was opened the following Day, when they were observed busied in forming a second Approach from the first, to a nearer Distance on the Road.

At Noon the French Fleet again came in View, much disabled, and anchored off the Port, where it continued 'till the 22d, when it finally disappeared.

This Day the Rebels were constructing Two other Batteries much lower down the Hill than the former, one on the Right for Five, the other on the Left of Green End Road for Seven Guns, both which were opened the next Day, when I found it necessary to attempt silencing them, and therefore ordered a Battery for Seven heavy Guns, on commanding Ground, near Green End, which, from the Obstructions given by the Enemy's Fire, could not be completed 'till the 25th, when the Rebels thought proper to close the Embrasures of their lower Batteries, and make Use of them for Mortars. During this Time they had been constructing on the Height of the East Road, another for One of Thirteen Inches; and this Day began a Third Approach in Front, and to the Right of their lower Batteries.

---

58 **Abatis.** An obstacle placed in an enemy's line of advance, comprised of felled trees with intertwined branches with the trunks parallel to the line of march.

59 **Fomini Hill** This is a spelling error for **Tomony Hill**, the 121-foot-high hill on the northwest side of Newport.

The 26th, observing the Enemy to discontinue their Works, and learning, from Deserters, they were removing the Officers Baggage and Heavy Artillery, I detached Lieutenant Colonel Bruce,[60] with a Hundred Men of the 54th Regiment, in the Night over Easton's Beach in Quest of Intelligence, who with great Address surprised and brought off a Piquet of Two Officers and Twenty-five Men, without any Loss. Some of Colonel Fanning's Corps,[61] at different Times, exerted themselves in taking off People from the Enemy's advanced Posts; but little Intelligence to be depended upon was ever obtained from them; nor were other Attempts to procure it more efficacious, as from all that could be learned, it was doubtful whether their Intentions were to attack our Lines or retreat.

On the 27th the *Sphynx*[62] and Two other Ships of War arrived; and I had the Honour of being informed by Colonel Stuart of your Excellency's Intention to reinforce this Post.

On the following Day the *Vigilant* Galley[63] took a Station to cover the Left Flank of the Army; and at Ten o'Clock that Night the Rebels made an Attempt to surprize a Subaltern's Piquet from the Anspach Corps, but were repulsed, after killing One Man, and wounding Two others.

---

60 **Andrew Bruce** was born in Scotland in 1742, the son of Sir Michael Bruce, who commanded the Stirlingshire Militia in 1745. He was commissioned an Ensign in the new-raising 56th Foot in England (renumbered 54th in 1757). He was promoted to 1st Lieutenant, in the new-raising 85th Foot in England on 9 June 1759, by raising for rank. He became Captain in the 85th Foot in 22 December 1761 by purchase vice a retirement. He went onto the British Half Pay List when his regiment disbanded on 24 May 1763. He transferred from Half Pay as Captain in the 38th Foot in Ireland on 14 February 1765. He was promoted to Major in the 38th Foot on 25 July 1771 by purchase. He became Lieutenant-Colonel in the 54th Foot while serving in Rhode Island on 10 March 1777, by purchase. He was promoted to Brevet Colonel on 20 November 1782. He died on 12 December 1791 at Naples, Italy, after 34.3 years' service.

61 This was the loyalist, King's American Regiment. **Edmund Fanning** was an American from New York, born in 1737. Before the Revolution, he had been Colonel of the Orange County Militia in North Carolina. In December 1776, General Howe appointed him Colonel of the King's American Regiment. He was wounded at Rhode Island in 1778. In 1779, he became Colonel and Commandant of the Rhode Island Loyal Associated Refugees. On Christmas Day 1782, he was reappointed Colonel of the King's American Regiment and went on to Half Pay as a Colonel in 1783. He served as Lieutenant-Governor of Nova Scotia from 24 February 1783 to 20 May 1786, then served as Lieutenant-Governor of St. John's Island (Prince Edward Island) from 4 November 1786 to 10 May 1804 and was Commandant, Island of St John Volunteers of the Royal Canadian Militia from 25 June 1795 to 24 June 1798. He was promoted to Major-General on 12 October 1793, and then to Lieutenant-General on 26 June 1799, and General on 25 April 1808. He died in London on 28 February 1818.

62 The 20-gun frigate **Sphinx**, was the lead ship in the Sphinx Class, commanded by Captain Alexander Graeme.

63 The 22-gun **Vigilant** was the former merchant ship *Empress of Russia* that the Admiralty had purchased in 1777 and designated a Sixth Rate, under the command of Commander Brabazon Christian.

The 29[64], at Break of Day, it was perceived that the Enemy had retreated during the night, upon which Major-General Prescott[64] was ordered to detach a Regiment from the second Line under this Command, over Easton's Beach, towards the left Flank of the Enemy's Encampment, and a Part of Brown's Corps was directed to take Possession of their Works. At the same Time Brigadier-General Smith[65] was detached with the 22[d] and 43[d] Regiments, and the Flank Companies of the 38th and 54th, by the East Road. Major-General Lossberg[66] marching by the West Road, with the Hessian

---

64 **Richard Prescott** was born in Ireland in 1725. He purchased a commission as a 2nd Lieutenant in the 32nd Regiment of Foot in Flanders. After being wounded in the arm at Fontenoy on 11 May 1745—a wound that never fully healed—he was promoted by purchase to Captain in the 33rd Foot in Flanders on 21 May 1746. He became a Major in the 1st Battalion, 33rd Foot on 20 December 1756, by purchase. He transferred, with his previous commission as Major, in the 72nd Foot when the 2nd Battalion of the 33rd Foot regimented as the 72nd Foot in the Spring of 1758. On 11 December 1759, he became a Major in the 50th Foot in England. He became Brevet Lieutenant-Colonel on 22 January 1761, then Lieutenant-Colonel in the 50th Foot on 22 May 1761, by a free death-vacancy. He became Lieutenant-Colonel in the 7th Foot at Gibraltar on 19 November 1761. Made a Brevet Colonel on 2 June 1772, he was deployed to Canada in 1773. After the American attack on Montreal in 1775, he led an attempt to reach Quebec. He surrendered to American forces under General Montgomery on 17 November 1775 and was made a prisoner. In September 1776, he was exchanged for Major-General John Sullivan. Returning to his regiment, he was given a local promotion to Major-General in America on 1 January 1776 and additionally Colonel of the 7th Foot on 12 November 1776. In December 1776, he became third in command for the expedition to Rhode Island. Promoted to Major-General in the Army, while in command at Rhode Island on 29 August 1777, he retained that position until he was captured by the Americans at Prescott Farm on 10 October 1777. Exchanged for General Charles Lee in April 1778, he briefly resumed his duties at Rhode Island before Sir Robert Pigot replaced him. Prescott was promoted to Lieutenant-General on 20 November 1782 and died on 20 October 1788 in London after 44.5 years' service. For details of his capture in 1777, see Christian M. McBurney, *Kidnapping the Enemy: Special Operations to capture Generals Charles Lee & Richard Prescott* (Yardley, PA: Westholme, 2014).

65 **Francis Smith** was born in England in 1723. He purchased a commission as Lieutenant in the 7th Regiment of Foot in Gibraltar on 25 March 1741. He was promoted to Captain in the 10th Foot in Gibraltar on 22 June 1747, by purchase. He became a Major in the 10th Foot on 25 September 1758, a free death vacancy. He was made Brevet Lieutenant-Colonel on 16 January 1762, then Lieutenant-Colonel in the 10th Foot on 13 February 1762, by purchase. He commanded at Lexington and Concord in April 1775. During the retreat to Boston he was wounded in the thigh. He was promoted to Brevet Colonel, 8 September 1775 and then obtained a local temporary promotion to Brigadier-General in America, before being promoted to Major-General on 19 February 1779. He became Colonel of the 11th Foot on 10 August 1781. Smith was promoted to Lieutenant-General on 28 September 1787. He died on 7 November 1791 in his home in Lower Grosvenor Street, London, after 50.6 years' service.

66 **Friedrich Wilhelm von Loßberg** was born in Rinteln, Grafshaft Schaumburg, Hessen-Kassel in 1720. As a Colonel, he was sent to America in command of the Fusilier Regiment von Loßberg (Alt). The regiment was placed in the second division of Hessian Troops commanded by Lieutenant General Wilhelm Freiherr von Knyphausen. On 7 December 1776, Colonel von Loßberg and his regiment were among the British and Hessian troops that landed at Newport under General Clinton. In May 1778, von Loßberg was promoted to Major-General and was second in command of the Newport garrison. With the departure from America of Lieutenant-General von Knyphausen on 15 May 1782, together with Lieutenant General Sir Henry Clinton, von Loßberg became the Commander of the Hessian Troops in North America, under Lieutenant General Sir Guy Carleton. Von Loßberg departed America in 1783 for Hesse, where he died in 1800.

Chasseurs[67] and the Anspach Regiments of Voit and Seaboth, in order, if possible, to annoy them in their Retreat; and upon receiving a Report from General Smith, that the Rebels made a Stand, and were in Force upon Quaker's Hill. I ordered the 54th and Hessian Regiment of Huyn, with Part of Brown's Corps, to sustain him; but before they could arrive, the Perseverance of General Smith, and the spirited Behaviour of the Troops, had gained Possession of the strong Post on Quaker's Hill, and obliged the Enemy to retire to their Works at the North End of the Island. On hearing a smart Fire from the Chasseurs engaged on the West Road, I dispatched Colonel Fanning's Corps of Provincials to join General Lossberg, who obliged the Rebels to quit two Redoubts made to cover their Retreat, drove them before him, and took Possession of Turkey Hill. Towards Evening, an Attempt being made by the Rebels to surround and cut off the Chasseurs, who were advanced on the Left, the Regiments of Fanning and Huyn were ordered up to their Support, and, after a smart Engagement with the Enemy, obliged them to retreat to their main Body of Windmill Hill.

---

67 **Chasseurs.** "During the war, the Hessians organized four provisional companies of chasseurs to serve as light infantry during a campaign. The officers and men were selected from the regiments. Unlike the Jägers, who were often called chasseurs, the men in the chasseur companies were infantrymen armed with regular muskets and bayonets rather than rifles carried by the Jägers. The first two companies were formed in December 1776 at Rhode Island. Twenty-five men were selected from each of the six Hessian regiments participating in the attack on the island. These were the Regiments Leib, Prinz Carl, von Ditfourth, von Wutginau, von Huyn, and von Bünau. The first commander of the chasseurs was Staff Captain Johann George Seelig of the Regiment Prinz Carl followed by Staff Captain Ludwig Eggerding of the Fusilier Regiment von Ditfourth and Second Lieutenant Friedrich Gombert of the Garrison Regiment von Bünau. By mid-July 1777 they were succeeded by Captain Friedrich Wilhelm von der Malsburg and Staff Captain August Christian Noltenius of the same regiments as their predecessors. Each man was to receive a blanket and cloth to make a pair of leggings. On 6 May 1777, the chasseurs of the Leib and Prinz Carl Regiments were ordered to immediately rejoin their regiments, which were returning to New York. The chasseurs of the Regiment Landgraf (previously named von Wutginau) rejoined their regiment in June 1779 when that regiment was recalled to New York. The companies were disbanded when the British evacuated Rhode Island in October 1779 and returned to New York." Donald M. Londahl-Smidt, *German Troops in the American Revolution (1) Hessen Cassel* (Oxford: Osprey, 2021), p. 41.

To these Particulars I am in Justice obliged to add Brigadier-General Smith's Report, who, amidst the general Tribute due to the good Conduct of every Individual under his Command, has particularly distinguished Lieutenant-Colonel Campbell[68] and the 22ᵈ Regiment, on whom, by their Position, the greater Weight of the Action tell. He also mentions with Applause the spirited Exertions of Lieutenant-Colonel Marsh[69] and the 43ᵈ Regiment, of Captains Coore[70] and Trench,[71] who commanded the Flank Companies. He likewise acknowledges particular Obligations to all the Officers and Men of the Royal Artillery, as also to the Seamen who were attached to the Field Pieces; and has expressed his

---

68 **John Campbell** was born in England in 1731. He was commissioned an Ensign in the 22ⁿᵈ Regiment of Foot at Minorca on 14 December 1746, probably by purchase, vice a retirement. He was promoted to Lieutenant in the 22ⁿᵈ Foot on 21 January 1755 in a free death-vacancy. He became a Captain-Lieutenant in the 22ⁿᵈ Foot on 5 July 1758, by purchase and then purchased a commission as a Captain on 26 May 1760. He became a Major in the 22ⁿᵈ Foot on 21 April 1768, by purchase. He was promoted to Lieutenant-Colonel in the 22ⁿᵈ Foot on 24 June 1775 in a free dd-vacancy. Campbell retired on 11 October 1778. Four years after retiring from regimental service, he was appointed Lieutenant-Governor of Plymouth, a post held until his death in 1804. While in Plymouth, he was made Captain of late John Pigot's Plymouth Invalid Company on 28 May 1788 and served until his death, having a total of 47.9 years' service.

69 **James Marsh** was born in England in 1733. He purchased a commission as an Ensign in the 46ᵗʰ Foot in Ireland on 9 February 1750/1. He was promoted to Lieutenant in the 46ᵗʰ Foot on 20 June 1753, by purchase. He served as adjutant of his regiment from 22 January 1755 to 22 April 1757. He was promoted to Captain in the 46ᵗʰ Foot on 2 February 1757, by purchase. He became a Brevet Major on 23 July 1772 and was promoted to Major in the 46ᵗʰ Foot on 20 February 1773, by purchase. He became a Lieutenant-Colonel in the 43ʳᵈ Foot in New York on 28 August 1776, he was made Brevet Colonel on 20 November 1782, then promoted to Colonel in the new-raising 77ᵗʰ Foot in Scotland on 12 October 1787, a regiment that embarked for the East Indies in the Spring of 1788). He was promoted to Major-General on 12 October 1793, and then to Lieutenant-General on 1 January 1798 and to General on 25 September 1803. He died on 15 June 1804, after 53.4 years' service.

70 **Thomas Coore** was born in England in 1744. He was commissioned a Lieutenant in Capt. Alexander Wood's new-raising Independent Company, one of thirty-five then raising in Great Britain, on 28 October 1760. He went in the same commission with Company when it was amalgamated with others, in January-February 1761, to form Sir Charles Grey's 98ᵗʰ Foot. Coore went onto British Half Pay when the regiment disbanded on 14 November 1763. He transferred from Half Pay as a Lieutenant in the 54ᵗʰ Foot at Gibraltar on 18 May 1764, He was promoted to Captain in the 54ᵗʰ Foot in Ireland on 16 August 1770, by purchase. He became a Major in the 28ᵗʰ Foot at New York on 6 October 1778, by purchase. He promoted to Lieutenant-Colonel in the 86ᵗʰ Foot in the Leeward Islands on 13 October 1780, by purchase. He retired on 4 April 1783, after 22 years' service.

71 **Eyre Power Trench** was born in Ireland in 1749, the son of Colonel Richard Trench (1710-1768), a Member of the Irish Parliament for County Galway. His elder brother was William Power Keating Trench, 1st Earl of Clancarty. He became Coronet in the 14ᵗʰ Dragoons in Ireland on 13 April 1768, by purchase. He was promoted to Lieutenant in the 14ᵗʰ Dragoons on 12 December 1770, by purchase. He became a Captain in the 54ᵗʰ Foot in Ireland on 1 December 1775, by purchase, and then a Major in the 38ᵗʰ Foot in New England on 8 September 1781, also by purchase. He was made a Brevet Lieutenant-Colonel on 18 November 1790, then commissioned Lieutenant-Colonel Commandant of his own new-raising 102ⁿᵈ Regiment of Foot in Ireland on 31 October 1793. He was made Brevet Colonel on 21 August 1795, then promoted to Colonel in the 102ⁿᵈ Foot on 1 September 1795, shortly before the 102ⁿᵈ was disbanded. He married Charlotte Frances Johnstone, daughter of General unknown Johnstone, in 1797 and became a Major-General on 18 July 1798, a Lieutenant-General on 30 October 1805. He died on 29 July 1808, after 40.2 years' service.

Thanks to Captain Barry,[72] of the 52ᵈ Regiment, who was a Volunteer on this Occasion, and assisted in carrying his Orders. General Losberg has given his Testimony of the very good Behaviour of the Anspach Corps, commanded by Colonel de Voit, and of Captains Malsburg[73] and Noltenius, with their Companies of Chasseurs.

After these Actions, the Enemy took Post in great Numbers on Windmill Hill, and employed themselves in strengthening that advantageous Situation.

This Night the Troops lay on their Arms on the Ground they had gained, and Directions were given for bringing up the Camp Equipage. Artillery were likewise sent for and Preparation made to remove the Rebels from their Redoubts; but by means of the great Number of Boats, they retreated in the Night of the 30ᵗʰ over Bristol and Howland's Ferry; thus relinquishing every Hold on the Island, and resigning to us its entire Possession.

During these tedious and fatiguing Operations, I was much indebted to the active Zeal of Captain Brisbane[74] and all the Captains, other Officers and Men of the Navy, who enabled me to man the different Batteries with their most experienced Officers, and best Men, who by their Example and constant Attention contributed much in the Support of the Defences. And I must also take Notice of the good Inclination for the Service, shewn by the Marines of the different Ships, which occasioned

---

72 **Henry Barry** was born in England in 1749/50. The son of Captain Robert Barry and his wife Sarah, of Worcester, Henry Barry was commissioned as 2ⁿᵈ Lieutenant in the 85ᵗʰ regiment of Foot in Portugal on 22 February 1763, a free vacancy. He went onto the British Half Pay List when the regiment disbanded on 24 May 1763. On 11 March 1768. he transferred to the 52ⁿᵈ Foot as an Ensign at Quebec. There, he was promoted to Lieutenant in the 52ⁿᵈ Foot on 23 September 1772, by purchase. Barry was commissioned in a provincial captaincy of 26 December 1775 in the new-raising Loyal Nova Scotia Volunteers, but he resigned from it shortly before 12 May 1776. In this period, he wrote an anonymous pamphlet on the advantages that Americans gained from the British imperial connection and another on the strength of British military and naval power. After his regimental promotion to Captain-Lieutenant in the 52ⁿᵈ Foot on 4 January 1777, by purchase and his Army promotion to Captain on 8 May 1777, the 52ⁿᵈ Foot, then under strength, returned to Britain for recruiting duty in late 1778. Barry returned to America in 1780 as deputy to Colonel Francis, Lord Rawdon, the Adjutant-General of British Forces in America. With Rawdon in South Carolina, he was credited with writing the best dispatches sent to the ministry in London. At the Battle of Eutaw Springs in September 1781, American forces captured Barry and held him as a prisoner of war until March 1782. Following a brief return to England, he was made a Brevet Lieutenant-Colonel during the Second Anglo-Mysore War. on 13 June 1782, then he became a Brevet Major in the Army on 19 February 1783. He remained in India for some time after the peace but had returned to England by 1787. He was promoted to Lieutenant-Colonel in the 39ᵗʰ Foot in Ireland on 8 December 1790. He resigned on 31 March 1793 with 25.3 years of service, but was then promoted to Colonel on 19 July 1793, then joined Major-General Francis Rawdon-Hastings, Lord Moira, on his expedition to Ostend in June-July 1794. Thereafter, Barry retired to Bath, where he was socially active. He died at Bath on 2 November 1822. The regiment, with the 36ᵗʰ Foot, embarked at Portsmouth, for the East Indies in March 1783, where it remained until March 1798.

73 **Friedrich Wilhelm von der Malsburg** was born in 1745. He served as staff captain in the Hessen-Kassel Fusilier Regiment von Ditfurth.

74 **John Brisbane**, born in Renfrewshire, Scotland in 1735, was the senior naval officer at Newport during this period and in command of the 32-gun frigate *Flora* from December 1775 until he ordered her scuttled at Newport on 5 August 1778 to avoid capture. He had commissioned a Lieutenant on 5 August 1751, and was promoted to Captain on 24 September 1761. He retired from active service in December 1781, but eventually rose by seniority on the retired list to Admiral of the Red in November 1805. He died on 10 September 1807.

my giving them in Charge the Defence of that principal Post on Fomini Hill. Nor can I conclude this Account, without expressing my sincere Acknowledgments to every Officer and Soldier under my Command, and to the several Departments, for their unwearied Exertions to counteract so many Difficulties.

The Prisoners taken on the 29th are not many in Number; but I have Reason to believe the Killed and Wounded of the Rebels is greater than that in the Return I have the Honor to inclose you of ours.

Return of the Killed, Wounded, and Missing, of the Troops under the Command of Major-General Sir Robert Pigot. Rhode Island, August 29, 1778

Flank Companies, 38th, 54th. 1 Serjeant killed; 1 Lieutenant, 1 Serjeant, 1 Drummer, 19 Rank and File, wounded; 1 Lieutenant, 2 Rank and File, missing.

22d Regiment. 11 Rank and File killed; 1 Lieutenant, 3 Ensigns, 2 Serjeants, 48 Rank and File, wounded; 1 Rank and File missing.

43d Regiment. 1 Serjeant, 2 Rank and File, killed; 2 Ensigns, 14 Rank and File, wounded; 1 Rank and File missing.

Royal Artillery. 1 Serjeant, 2 Rank and File, 1 Driver, killed; 1 Lieutenant, 10 Rank and File, 2 Drivers, wounded.

Huyn's Regiment. 1 Captain, 4 Rank and File, killed; 1 Captain, 5 Serjeants, 51 Rank and File, wounded, 1 Serjeant, 5 Rank and File, missing.

1st Battalion Anspach. 2 Rank and File killed: 3 Rank and File wounded.

2d Battalion ditto. 4 Rank and File killed; 1 Serjeant, 5 Rank and File, wounded.

Hessian Chasseurs. 2 Rank and File killed; 1 Captain, 1 Lieutenant, 1 Serjeant, 14 Rank and File, wounded; 1 Rank and File missing.

Hessian Artillery. 1 Serjeant wounded.

King's American Regiment. 1 Volunteer, 1 Serjeant, 3 Rank and File, killed; 1 Lieutenant, 2 Ensigns, 2 Serjeants, 15 Rank and File, wounded.

Seamen. 1 killed; 1 wounded.

Total. 1 Captain, 1 Volunteer, 4 Serjeants, 31 Rank and File, 1 Driver, killed. 2 Captains, 5 Lieutenants, 7 Ensigns, 13 Serjeants, 1 Drummer, 180 Rank and File, 2 Drivers, wounded. 1 Lieutenant, 1 Serjeant, 10 Rank and File, missing.

(Signed)   R. PIGOT.

Names of the Officers killed, wounded and missing.

Flank Companies. Lieutenant Swiney,[75] 38th, Prisoner. Lieutenant Layard,[76] 54th, wounded.

---

[75] **Shapland Swiney** (or Swinny) was born in Ireland in 1756. He was commissioned Ensign in the 38th regiment of Foot in Ireland on 26 September 1772, by purchase. He was promoted to Lieutenant in the 38th Foot on 4 May 1776, by purchase. He transferred onto the British Half Pay List on 14 December 1785, after 13.3 years' service. He was still on Half Pay in 1820, but his name was removed from the List in 1821.

[76] **John Thomas Layard** was born in England in 1753, the second son of Susanne Henriette de Boisragon and Daniel Peter Layard, (1720-1805), MD, DCL, FRS, FSA, physician to HRH Augusta, Princess of Wales. His younger brother was Anthony Lewis Layard. He was commissioned an Ensign in the 54th Regiment of Foot in Ireland on 21 June 1772, by purchase. He was promoted to Lieutenant in the 54th Foot on 7 July 1775, by purchase vice a retirement. He was made Brevet Captain on 1 July 1783 in unknown circumstances. He was promoted to the regimental rank of Captain-Lieutenant of the 54th Foot on 24 August 1787, probably by purchase, vice an augmentation. He received his Army promotion to Captain in the 54th Foot on 1 August 1792, by purchase. He was made Brevet Major on 1 March 1794, then Major in the 54th Foot on 1 September 1795. He became Brevet Lieutenant-Colonel on 1 January 1798, then Lieutenant-Colonel in the 54th Foot on 16 May 1800 and Brevet Colonel on 25 April 1803. He was promoted to Major-General on 4 June 1811. He was reduced onto Half Pay in 1814 and promoted to Lieutenant-General on 19 July 1821. He died at Bath, on 22 May 1828 after 34.5 years' service.

22d Regiment. Lieutenant Cleghorn,[77] Ensigns Borland,[78] Proctor,[79] and Adam,[80] wounded.

43d Regiment. Ensigns Roche[81] and Affleck[82] wounded.

---

77 **George Cleghorn** was born in Scotland in 1759. A Gentleman Volunteer with army, he was made an Ensign in the 22nd Regiment of Foot in New England on 24 July 1775 by purchase. He was promoted to Lieutenant in the 22nd Foot on 13 January 1777, by purchase. He promoted to Captain in the 38th Foot in New York on 26 June 1780, by purchase. He retired on 28 February 1792 with 16.6 years' service.

78 **John Lindall Borland** was born in Boston, Massachusetts in 1753/54. Commissioned an Ensign in the 22nd Foot in New England on 24 November 1775, by purchase, he was promoted Lieutenant in the 22nd Foot on, 14 August 1778, by purchase. He transferred onto the British Half Pay List on 5 July 1786, the transferred from Half Pay as Lieutenant in the 10th Foot in Jamaica on 24 March 1790. He transferred again as Lieutenant in the 19th Foot in England on 11 May 1791. He was promoted to Captain in the 38th Foot in Ireland on 28 February 1792, by purchase. He became a Major in the 38th Foot on 18 October 1797 in a a free death-vacancy. He was made Brevet Lieutenant-Colonel on 29 April 1802 and then retired on 9 April 1807after 27.7 years' service. As a widower, he married Elizabeth Dyland on 14 November 1814 at St Marylebone, Westminster, London. He died in London on 16 November 1825.

79 **William Proctor** was born in Massachusetts in 1755. Proctor joined the 65th Regiment of Foot in America as a Gentleman Volunteer and received a provincial commission as a 2nd Lieutenant on 1 August 1775 in the new-raising loyalist Royal Fencible Americans. He left this unit for a regular commission, probably by purchase, in the 22nd Regiment of Foot in which he became an Ensign on 7 August 1776 at New York. He died on 19 September 1778 of the wounds he suffered on 29 August 1778, after 2.1 years' service.

80 **Andrew Adam** was commissioned an Ensign in the 22nd Foot in New England on 18 January 1777 in a free vacancy. He died on 6 September 1778 of wounds on 29 August 1778, after 1.7 years' service.

81 **Winthrop Roche** was born in Ireland in 1758. He was commissioned an Ensign in the 46th Regiment of Foot at Quebec on 27 October 1775 in a free augmentation vacancy. He became an Ensign in the 43rd Foot in New England on 23 November 1775 and was then promoted to Lieutenant in the 43rd Foot on 17 October 1778, by purchase. He was promoted to the regimental rank of Captain-Lieutenant in the 43rd Foot on 27 April 1787, by purchase, and later received his Army commission as Captain in the 43rd Foot on 24 September 1787 in a free augmentation vacancy. He retired on 30 April 1792 with 16.5 years' service.

82 **James Affleck** was born in England in 1759. He purchased a commission as an Ensign in the 43rd Regiment of Foot in Ireland on 29 February 1776, just as the regiment was embarking for America. He was promoted to Lieutenant of the 43rd Foot on 9 December 1778, by purchase. While at New York, he was promoted to Captain in the 26th Foot on 15 September 1779, by purchase. On 16 January 1782, he transferred to the newly raising 23rd Light Dragoons in England, obtaining the regimental rank of Captain-Lieutenant before the regiment sailed for India in early 1782. He was promoted to Captain in the 23rd Light-Dragoons on 2 March 1785 by purchase. In 1786, his regiment was renumbered as the 19th Light Dragoons, just before he was promoted to Major in that regiment on 6 December 1786. He became a Brevet Lieutenant-Colonel on 1 March 1794 and received his promotion to Lieutenant-Colonel in the 16th Light Dragoons on 25 March 1795. He then became Brevet Colonel on 1 January 1798. He was promoted to Major-General on 1 January 1805. In 1808, he succeeded as 3rd Baronet to the Affleck Baronetcy of Dulham Hall in Suffolk. He was promoted to Lieutenant-General on 4 June 1811 and to General on 27 May 1825. He died on 10 August 1833, still shown in his Lieutenant-Colonel's rank in the 16th Light Dragoons, after 57.4 years' service!

Royal Artillery. Second Lieutenant Kemble[83] wounded.

Huyn's Regiment. Captain Schallern[84] killed. Captain Wagener[85] wounded.

Hessian Chasseurs. Captain Noltenius,[86] *Bunanu's Regiment*, Lieutenant Murarius,[87] *Langrave's,* wounded.

---

83 This appears to be a typographical error as there were no officers named Kemble in the Royal Artillery at this time; it is likely a reference to **William Pemble**. Born in England in 1756, Pemble was appointed Cadet at Royal Military Academy, Woolwich, on 2 Aril 1771 and became a 2nd Lieutenant in the Royal Artillery on 1 December 1775. Then, he purchased a commission as Lieutenant in the 26th Regiment of Foot at New York on 2 November 1778. He became Captain-Lieutenant in the 104th Foot in England on 6 March 1782 in a free augmentation vacancy. He transferred as a Captain in Captain Thomas Dunbar's North British Invalid Company on 5 February 1783, and then as Captain in the late Captain George Coote's Landguard Fort Invalid Company, 22 June 1785. Following the disbandment of the fourteen invalid companies in 1791, he was listed as Captain, "late British Invalid Companies" from 23 March 91, with 15.3 years' service. His name was removed from the Half Pay List in 1830.

84 **George Friedrich von Schallern** was from Neustadt an der Aisch, Brandenburg-Bayreuth. He was commissioned in Hessen-Kassel's Garnison Regiment von Huyn on 17 August 1769. The October 1777 *Rang Liste* listed him for first time as Captain, having been given command of the vacant Wagner company, his predecessor having died in New York on 12 March 1777. Von Schallern was killed in Rhode Island on 29 August 1778.

85 **Carl Wegner** was from Trendelburg in Hessen-Kassel. He was Second Lieutenant, Hessen-Kassel's Garnison Regiment von Huyn on 10 March 1761. He was promoted to First Lieutenant, Garnison Regiment von Huyn on 15 January 1776. Wegner was wounded in the leg on 29 August 1778 and died in Newport, Rhode Island on 23 September 1778.

86 **August Christian Noltenius** was from Nordeck in Hessen-Kassel. He was commissioned a Staff Captain in the Hessen-Kassel Garnison Regiment von Bünau on 17 February 1776. Noltenius was wounded in the left side on 29 August 1778.

87 **Ludwig Eberhard Murarius** was commissioned a First Lieutenant in Hessen-Kassel's Regiment Landgraf on 9 May 1776. He was wounded on Windmill Hill in Rhode Island on 29 August 1778. On 15 April 1779, he was promoted to Staff Captain, in the Regiment Landgraf.

King's American Regiment. Lieutenant Campbell,[88] Ensigns Eastick[89] and Purdy,[90] wounded.

Volunteer Eustace,[91] *King's American Regiment*, killed.

(Signed)   R. PIGOT.

Admiralty Office, October 27, 1778.

The Dispatches from Vice-Admiral Lord Viscount Howe, Commander in Chief of His Majesty's Ships in North America, to Mr. Stephens,[92] of which the following are Extracts, were brought to this Office on Sunday last by Lieutenant Grove, of His Majesty's Ship the *Apollo*, which Ship left New York the 17th of last Month, and arrived at Plymouth the 22d Instant.

---

88 **Dugald Campbell** became an Ensign in the North Carolina Provincials on 14 February 1776. He was present at the Battle of Moore's Creek Bridge on 27 February 1776. By order of Governor Joseph Martin and General Howe, he was seconded to New York and his subsistence as an engineer was paid at the rate of a Lieutenant between February and November 1776. He was promoted to Lieutenant in the King's American Regiment on 29 January 1776. Wounded at Rhode Island in 29 August 1778. He served as a Lieutenant in the provisional cavalry troop of the King's American Regiment from June 1781 to July 1782. He was listed as Lieutenant, in the King's American Regiment on December 1782, but during 1783 went on Half Pay. He returned to military service on 24 October 1795 as a Captain in the New Brunswick Provincial Regiment and served until 24 August 1802. On 28 July 1803, he became a Captain in the Canadian Regiment of Fencible Infantry. On 8 December 1804, he exchanged as a Lieutenant in the 27th Regiment of Foot.

89 **Eastick** is a misspelling for **Stephen Hustice**, who obtained a warrant as an infantry Lieutenant in the Queen's American Rangers on 12 November 1776. In August 1777, he became an Ensign in the King's American Regiment, then on 12 October 1777, a Lieutenant. He was wounded in Rhode Island on 29 August 1778. On 25 December 1782, he was still a Lieutenant in the King's American Regiment. From 1783, he was a Half-Pay Provincial Lieutenant. In 1784, he signed a petition with others to Governor Parr to establish a town at St Ann's Point on the St. Johns River. He died at Parrsboro, Nova Scotia, on 26 January 1786.

90 **David Purdy** was a carpenter by trade, who was born on 3 December 1753. In 1775, he resided in New York. On 18 September 1777, General Howe gave him a commission as an Ensign in the King's American Regiment. After being wounded in Rhode Island on 29 August 1778, he was later promoted to Lieutenant in the King's American Regiment on 25 December 1782, He was a Half-Pay Lieutenant in 1783. He died in Queen's County, New York, on 21 March 1826.

91 Volunteer **Eustace,** first name unknown, died at Newport, Rhode Island on 29 August 1778. He was a nephew of Lieutenant-Colonel George Campbell (1732-1799) of the King's American Regiment.

92 **Philip Stephens**, Secretary of the Admiralty, 18 June 1763 to 13 January 1783, then First Secretary of he Admiralty 13 January 1783 to 3 March 1795.

Eagle, off Sandy Hook, August 17, 1778.

In Consequence of the Determination signified in my Letter of the 31st past, and the Intelligence I had subsequently received, that the French Squadron was separated into different Detachments, stationed off of the Entrance of the Middle Channel, and in the Narraganset and Seakonet Passages, for the Attack of Rhode Island, I attempted sailing from Sandy Hook the 2d Instant, with the Ships of War and attendant Vessels named in the annexed List, to profit by any Opportunity which might offer for taking Advantage of the Enemy in that divided Situation, and for the Relief, in that Case, of the Garrison at Newport; but the Wind veering back to the Southward, and not afterwards corresponding sooner with the rising of the Tide upon the Bar, my Departure was necessarily postponed until the Morning of the 6th; and I anchored the Squadron off of Point Judith the Evening of the 9th.

The Toulon Squadron[93] had passed the Batteries at the Entrance of the Harbour the preceding Day, and was mostly placed close over to the Conanicut Shore, in the middle Channel from Race Island Northward towards Dyers and Prudence Islands.

Being thereby enabled to communicate immediately with the Garrison, I was informed by Captain Brisbane of the Progress of the Enemy's Operations, together with the Destruction of the Frigates, and other Particulars since the Dates of his earlier Reports, as stated in the Copies of his several Letters herewith inclosed. By an Officer from the Major General Sir Robert Pigot I was at the same Time advised, that he had been obliged to evacuate Conanicut, as well as all his Out-posts on the Northern Parts of Rhode Island, and to confine his Defence to the Lines constructed on the Heights adjacent to the Town of Newport. Under these Circumstances I judged it was impracticable to afford the General any essential Relief.

The Wind changing to the North-East next Morning, the French Admiral stood out of the Port with the Twelve Two-decked Ships of his Squadron,[94] named in the List transmitted with your Letter dated the 3d of May.

Deeming the Superiority of the Enemy's Force too great to come to Action with them, if it could be avoided, whilst they possessed the Weather-gage, I steered with the Squadron formed in Order of Battle to the Southward, in the Hope of Having the Wind in from the Sea, as, by the Appearance of

---

93 **D'Estaing's squadron** was based at Toulon, France, on the Mediterranean coast.

94 The list was not printed in this issue of the *Gazette*. These **twelve French ships** of the line were the 80-gun flagship *Languedoc*, the 80-gun *Tonnant*, the 74-gun *César*, the 74-gun *Zélé*, the 74-gun *Hector*, the 74-gun *Guerrier*, the 74-gun *Marseillais*, the 74-gun *Protecteur*, the 64-gun *Vaillant*, the 64-gun *Provence*, the 64-gun *Fantasque*, and the 50-gun *Sagittaire*.

the Weather, was to be expected later in the Day: And, retaining the Fire-ships only, I sent Directions for the Bombs and Gallies to make Sail with the *Sphynx* for New York.

The Enemy being equally attentive to the same Object, no material Use could be made in an Alteration of the Wind, for a short Time, to the Southward of the East. I therefore continued the same Course the rest of the Day, under a Proportion of Sail for the *Phoenix, Experiment* and *Pearl,* having the three Fire-Ships in Tow, to keep Company with Facility: The French Ships advancing, though unequally, with all their Sail abroad.

The relative Position of the two Squadrons (about North and South from each other) remained the same on the Morning of the 11th; but by the Increase of Distance between them at Break of Day, it appeared that the Enemy had kept nearer the Wind during the Night, as their headmost Ships were then Hull down.[95]

The Wind continuing to the East North East, and having no further Expectation of being able to gain the Advantage of the Enemy with respect to it, as before proposed, I altered the Direction of the Ships by successive Changes of the Course in the same View; or, sailing still in that Attempt, to await the Approach of the Enemy, with the Squadron formed in Line of Battle ahead from the Wind to Starboard; and about Four in the Evening I made the Signal for the Ships to close to the Centre, when they shortened Sail accordingly. I had moved some Time before from the *Eagle* into the *Apollo,* to be better situated for directing the subsequent Operations of the Squadron.

The Rearing of the Enemy's Van (then under their Top-sails, between Two and Three Miles distant) was altered since the Morning from the East North-East to South South-East; and the French Admiral had formed his Line to engage the British Squadron to Leeward. He soon after bore away to the Southward, apparently from the State of the Weather; which, by the Wind freshening much with frequent Rain since the Morning, was now rendered very unfavourable for coming to Action with any suitable Effect.

The Wind increasing greatly that Night, and continuing violent with a considerable Sea until the Evening of the 13th, I was separated from the rest of the Squadron in the *Apollo,* (where I had been compelled by the Weather to remain) with the *Centurion, Ardent, Richmond, Vigilant, Roebuck,* and *Phoenix;* and, as I afterwards found, many of the other Ships had been also much dispersed.

The *Apollo's* Main-Mast being dangerously sprung in the Partners, which made it necessary to cut away the Top-Mast to save the Lower-Mast, and having lost her Fore-Mast in the Night of the Twelfth, I embarked in the *Phoenix,* when the Weather became more moderate later in the Day, to collect the

---

95 **Hull down** meaning that that the ship's hull was not visible, but that her masts and sails could still be seen on the horizon.

dispersed Ships, and sent the *Roebuck* (which had lost the Head of her Mizen-Mast) to attend the *Apollo* to Sandy Hook.

Having afterwards proceeded in the *Centurion* to the Southward, upon hearing several Guns on that Bearing in the Morning of the 15th, I discovered Ten-Sail of the French Squadron, some at Anchor in the Sea, about Twenty-five Leagues Eastward, from Cape May; leaving the *Centurion* thereupon, in a suitable Station, to direct any of the dispersed Ships, or those which might arrive of Vice-Admiral Byron's Squadron, after me, I repaired directly in the *Phoenix* for the appointed Rendezvous, and joined the rest of the Squadron, this Evening, off of Sandy Hook.

The Chief Damage sustained in the Squadron by the Effects of the late Gale of Wind, besides what I have before related, was confined to the *Cornwall* and *Raisonable*; the Main-Mast of the former, and Bowsprit of the last being sprung; but the *Cornwall's* Mast will soon be rendered serviceable. And the *Thunder* Bomb is still missing.

My Observations on the Ships of the French Squadron were confined solely to the Discovery of their Position. The Particulars of their Situation I have to add, were communicated by the different Commanders of His Majesty's Ships, which had been crossed earlier upon them.

The *Languedoc* and *Tonant* had lost all their Masts, the Main-Mast of the latter excepted. The *Languedoc* was met in that Condition in the Evening of the 13th, and attacked by the *Renown* with such Advantage, that the most happy Consequences might have been expected from Captain Dawson's resolute Efforts the next Morning, if the Execution of his Purpose had not been prevented by the Arrival of Six Sail of the French Squadron, which then joined the disabled Ship.

A similar Attempt, with the like Prospect of Success, was made the same Night by Commodore Hotham in the *Preston*, on the *Tenant*; and the Continuance of the Action, the next Morning, necessarily declined for the same Reason.

Neither of the Two Fifty-Gun Ships received any material Damage in those spirited Undertakings, besides the Loss of the *Preston's* Fore Yard, which is rendered very unserviceable.

One the 16th, the *Isis* was chased and engaged by a French Seventy-four-Gun Ship, bearing a Flag at the Mizen Top-Mast Head, and therefore supposed to be the *Zelé*. The Lords Commissioners will see in the Copy of the inclosed Report[96] from Captain Raynor,[97] the Event of that very unequal Contest. But it is requisite that I should supply the Deficiency of his Recital, by observing to their Lordships, that the Superiority acquired over the Enemy in the Action, appears to be not less an Effect of Captain Raynor's very skillful Management of his Ship, than of his distinguished Resolution, and the Bravery of his Men and Officers.

My chief Attention will be directed to a speedy Dispatch of the needful Repairs and Supplies in the Ships capable of being made soonest ready for Service. The *Experiment* has been ordered off of Rhode Island to procure Advices of the State of the Garrison at Newport; for the reducing of which the Rebels have been unavoidably left at Liberty to land any Force they many have drawn down to the adjacent Coasts, upon Rhode Island.

I am with great Consideration, &c.

HOWE

P. S. Since my Return to this Port, I have Received Letters from Captain Hawker, to acquaint me with the Loss of the *Mermaid,* which was forced on Shore near Senepuxen by the French Squadron, when the Enemy arrived first off the Delaware towards the Beginning of last Month.[98]

---

96 **The report** was not printed in this edition of the *Gazette.*

97 **Captain John Raynor** commanded the 50-gun *Isis* from 1778 to 1779. He was born about 1730 and joined the Royal Navy on 13 November 1747. He passed his Lieutenant's Examination on 19 December 1755 and was commissioned a Lieutenant on 26 February 1757. He was promoted to Commander on 1 July 1766 in command of the 14-gun ship sloop *Swift* until 1 June 1769. In 1767-1769, he was the senior British naval officer, while on patrol in the newly claimed Falkland Islands with the 14-gun *Tamar.* Promoted io captain on 26 July 1775, he commanded the 50-gun *Bristol,* flagship of Vice-Admiral Molyneux Shuldham on the North American Station. While in *Bristol,* he supervised the landings on Staten Island in 1776. In July 1777, he took command of *Isis* and was present at the Battle of St Lucia 14-15 December 1778. Then, he commanded the newly built 64-gun *Inflexible* from 14 February until his death on 25 August 1780.

98 On 8 July 1778, the French 50-gun *Fantasque,* commanded by one of the French Navy's most famous officers, Captain Pierre André, bailli de Suffren, in company with the 50-gun *Sagittaire,* commanded by comte d'Albert de Rions, chased the British 28-gun frigate *Mermaid.* To evade capture, Captain James Hawker ran her ashore. Some sources report that she was run ashore on Cape Henlopen or in Delaware Bay. *The Maryland Journal and Baltimore Advertiser* (21 July 1778) reports that she went ashore "near Chingoteague, where it is expected, she will be entirely lost. The whole Ship's Company are prisoners on the Eastern shore of this State." Howe's reference to Sinepuxent may refer to the inlet by that name that before 1818 was an opening through Assateague Island or to the Maryland village of Sinepuxent on Sinepuxent Neck across Sinepuxent Bay from the barrier island of Assateague and located just north and to seaward of Chincoteague Island in Virginia. The prisoners were sent to Philadelphia where they were eventually exchanged in Agust 1778.

List of the Squadron of His Majesty's Ships which sailed from Sandy Hook under the Command of the Vice-Admiral the Viscount Howe, August 6, 1778

THIRD RATE.

	Guns.	Men	
Eagle,	64	522	Vice-Admiral the Viscount Howe. – Captains Duncan[99] and Curtis.[100]

---

99 **Henry Duncan** was flag captain to Vice-Admiral Lord Howe from 1776 to 1782. Born in Scotland in about 1739, he initially served as a merchant seaman until he joined the Royal Navy as an able seaman on 10 May 1755 and served in the 64-gun *Nassau*. He was rated a Midshipman in 1756, he participated in the Louisburg expedition in 1757 and was present at the Battle of Lagos Bay, 18-19 August 1759. He passed his Lieutenant's Examination on 3 January 1759 and was commissioned a Lieutenant on 21 September 1759. Promoted to Commander on 26 May 1768, he commanded the 8-gun *Terror* in 1768-69, and then the 8-gun *Wasp,* in 1769-1772. He was promoted to Captain on 7 February 1776 to command the 64-gun *Eagle* until 1777. He served as Resident Commissioner at Halifax from 1783 to 1799, then was Resident Commissioner at Sheerness in 1800-1801, before becoming Deputy Controller of the Navy, 1801-1806. He died on 7 October 1814 at Dartmouth.

100 **Roger Curtis** commanded the 64-gun *Eagle* in succession to Henry Duncan, when Duncan moved up to be Howe's flag captain. Duncan remained in *Eagle* while she served as Howe's flagship until September 1778. Curtis was born at Downton, Wiltshire on 4 June 1746. He joined the Royal Navy in 1762. He passed his Lieutenant's Examination in 1769 and was commissioned a Lieutenant on 19 January 1771. Promoted to Commander on 11 July 1776, he commanded the 14-gun *Senegal* until he promoted to Captain on 30 April 1777 to command *Eagle*. On Half Pay until 1780, he commanded the 28-gun frigate *Brilliant* in which he was at Gibraltar 1780-1782. He commanded local naval forces during the Siege of Gibraltar, when he defended the fortress against Spanish floating batteries. In recognition of this action, he was appointed Knight Commander of the Bath. He commanded the 74-gun *San Miguel* in 1782-1784 and *Ganges* in 1784-1787. In 1790, he commanded the 100-gun *Queen Charlotte* and served as first captain to Admiral Lord Howe. Following the Battle of the Glorious First of June 1794, Curtis was promoted to Rear-Admiral and invested a Baronet. He was promoted to Vice-Admiral in 1799. In 1800-1803, he served as Commander in Chief at the Cape of Good Hope. On 23 April 1804, he was promoted to full Admiral and served on the board to revise the civil affairs of the Navy, 1805-1807. He presided over the court-martial of Admiral James Lord Gambier concerned the action at Basque Roads. He was appointed Knight Grand Cross of the Order of the Bath in 1815 and died at Gatcombe, Isle of Wight, on 14 November 1816.

Trident,	64	517	Commodore Elliot.[101] – Captain Molloy.[102]

---

101 **Captain John Elliot** commanded *Trident* from April 1777 until April 1778, when Captain Molloy relieved him. Thereafter Elliot flew his broad pennant as a Commodore commanding a division of Howe's fleet. Elliot was born in Scotland in April 1732, the fourth son of Sir George Elliot, 2nd Bart. (1693-1766). He joined the Royal Navy on 3 July 1746. He passed his Lieutenant's Examination on 1 May 1752 and was commissioned a Lieutenant through the influence of his eldest brother, George, then a Member of Parliament for Selkirkshire, on 30 April 1756. Promoted to Commander on 21 January 1757, he briefly commanded the 12-gun sloop *Mediterranean* and the 14-gun sloop *Albany* before being promoted to Captain on 5 April 1757 in command of the 28-gun frigate *Hussar*. He commanded five ships during the Seven Years' War and was present at the action of 19 March 1759, the action of 28 February 1760 that killed the French privateer François Thurot, and the expedition to Belle-Isle. Through his brother's influence, he became Member of Parliament for Cockermouth in 1767-1768. He stood for Carlisle in 1768 but was defeated and did not return to Parliament. He returned to sea in 1770-1771 in command of the 50-gun *Portland*. In January 1776, he was elected a Fellow of the Royal Society. In late 1778, he returned to England. In May 1779, he took command of the 74-gun *Edgar* and participated in Rodney's relief of Gibraltar and the Battle of Cape St Vincent in 1780, remaining in her until 1782-1783, when he briefly commanded the 50-gun *Romney*. Unemployed from the end of the war he became Governor and Commander-in-Chief of Newfoundland in 1786-89. He as promoted to Vice-Admiral in 1790, but soon retired. He returned to his home at Mount Teviot, Roxburghshire, where he was promoted on the retired list by seniority through the ranks to Admiral of the Red on 9 November 1805. He died at his home on 20 September 1808.

102 **Anthony James Pye Molloy** commanded *Trident* from 11 April 1778 until 23 July 1780. He was commissioned a Lieutenant on 3 August 1768, then promoted to Commander on 6 July 1776 in command of the 8-gun *Thunder*. He left *Thunder* on 11 November 1776, then took command of the 14-gun *Senegal* on 2 May 1777 until 11 April 1778, when he was promoted to Captain and took command of *Trident*. On leaving her, he commanded the 64-gun *Intrepid* at the Battle of Fort Royal, the Chesapeake, and St Kitts. After the war, he briefly commanded the 74-gun *Fortitude* in 1787, *Bombay Castle* in 1789-1790, *Edgar* in 1790-1792, and *Ganges* in 1792-1793. On 23 December 1793, he was appointed to command the 80-gun *Caesar* and was at the Battle of the Glorious First of June 1794. He was court martialed at Portsmouth on 28 April 1795 for failing to breach the French battle line in the battle and was dismissed from the service on 16 May 1795. He died 25 July 1814.

FOURTH RATE.

Preston,   50   367   Commodore Hotham.[103] – Captain Uppleby.[104]

---

103 **Commodore William Hotham** had sailed from England in June 1776, flying his broad pennant in *Preston*, escorting a convoy of transports carrying Hessian troops and a detachment of Guards. He remained in North American waters until 1781. Hotham was born on 8 April 1736 in York, the third son of Sir Beaumont Hotham (1698-1771), 7th Baronet of South Dalton and a Commissioner of the Customs. He attended Westminster School and then Royal [Naval] Academy at Portsmouth from 1748 to 1751. He entered the Navy as a Volunteer per Order in 1748. He passed his Lieutenant's Examination on 7 August 1754 and was commissioned 28 January 1755. His first assignment was to the flagship of Sir Edward Hawke, who he followed in several assignments and who prompted him to commander on 19 November 1756 in successive command of several sloops. After capturing a large French privateer, Hotham was promoted to captain on 17 August 1757, commanding in succession the 20-gun vessels *Gibraltar* and *Squirrel*, and then the 36-gun *Melampe*. After participating in the Belle Isle operation in 1761, he then took command of the 32-gun *Aeolus*. In 1766, he took command of the 74-gun *Hero* and then in 1770 *Resolution*. In 1774, he shifted his board pennant from *Preston* to the 44-gun *Phoenix*, then in 1780 to the 74-gun *Vengeance* in which he fought three engagements under Rodney with the French fleet. He was promoted to Rear-Admiral in 13 September 1787, then Vice-Admiral in 1790. In 1793, he served under Howe as second in command of the Mediterranean fleet and succeeded him in 1794. He resigned in 1797 and was raised to the peerage as Baron Hotham of South Dalton. Promoted to Admiral on the Retired List on 14 February 1799, he died on 2 May 1813 at South Dalton, Yorkshire.

104 **Captain Samuel Uppleby** commanded *Preston* from 8 April 1776 to 28 July 1779. Uppleby was born about 1733 and joined the Navy on 7 February 1747. He passed his Lieutenant's Examination on 16 January 1754. He was commissioned a Lieutenant on 9 November 1757 and was assigned to the 74-gun *Valiant* in 1763-64. Promoted to Commander in 2 June 1772, he commanded the 10-gun *Hawk* 8 April 1775. He was promoted to Captain on 8 April 1776 on taking command of *Preston*. After participating in the Rhode Island operations, he was at St Lucia in December 1778. He left *Preston* to take command of the 74-gun *Vengeance* on 28 July 1779 and remained in her until 17 January 1780, when he took command of the 36-gun frigate *Blanche*. He drowned on 11 October 1780, when his ship was lost with all hands in "the Great Hurricane" off Antigua.

THIRD RATE

Cornwall,	74	600	Captain Edwards.[105]
Nonsuch,	64	500	Captain Griffith.[106]
Raisonable,	64	500	Captain Fitzherbert.[107]
Somerset,	64	500	Captain Ourry.[108]

---

105 **Captain Timothy Edwards** commanded *Cornwall* from January 1778, Part of Byron's squadron, he had joined Howe on 30 July 1778. Edwards was born in 1731 in Nanhoran, North Wales, the son of the Rev'd William Edwards. He joined the Royal Navy in November 1745. He passed his Lieutenant's Examination on 19 June 1752 and was commissioned a Lieutenant on 6 February 1755. He was promoted to Commander on 16 November 1757 and placed in command of the 16-gun ship sloop *Favorite*. Promoted to Captain on 5 August 1759, he took command of the 28-gun frigate *Valeur* and served in her until 1 April 1761. He subsequently commanded the 32-gun *Emerald* in 1762-1763 and 64-gun *Europa* from 19 September 1777 to 23 January 1778, when he took command of *Cornwall*. He remained in command until his ship was scuttled and burnt at St Lucia on 30 June 1780, after being declared unserviceable following battle damage. He died of his wounds while a passenger in the frigate *Actaeon* on 12 July 1780.

106 **Captain Walter Griffith** had been in command of *Nonsuch* since February 1776. Griffith was born on 15 May 1727 and joined the Royal Navy in December 1743. He was the nephew of Captain Thomas Trevor (d. 1745), in whose ship, the 90-gun *Duke*, Griffith eventually became a Midshipman in 1748. He passed his Lieutenant's Examination on 30 April 1755 and was promoted to Lieutenant on 7 May 1755. Promoted to Commander on 4 June 1759, he successively commanded the 18-gun *Postillion* and the 20-gun *Gibraltar*. Promoted to Captain on 11 December 1759, he remained in command of Gibraltar until she was paid off in 1763. In 1770-1771, he commanded the 90-gun *Namur*, and was unemployed until taking command of *Nonsuch*. After leaving *Nonsuch* in late 1778, he took command of the 74-gun *Conqueror*. While commanding her during the Battle of Martinique on 18 December 1779, he was killed in action.

107 **Captain Thomas Fitzherbert** commanded *Raisonnable* from 2 February 1776 to 4 December 1778. Born in 1727, he joined the Royal Navy on 30 April 1739. He passed his Lieutenant's Examination on 25 Match 1752 and was commissioned a Lieutenant on 20 February 1755. Promoted to Commander on 14 March 1760, he commanded the 8-gun *Speedwell* in 1760-61 and then the 14-gun *Senegal*. He was promoted to Captain on 10 July 1761, commanding the 24-gun *Wager* until 14 March 1763. Thereafter, he commanded successively the 32-gun *Adventure* in 1766-1769, the 30-gun *Renown* in 1769-1770, the 60-gun *Conquestador* in 1773, and the 74-gun *Dublin* in 1773-1776. After leaving *Raisonnable*, he was on Half-Pay until 12 December 1779, when he was appointed to command the 74-gun *Royal Oak*. On 11 May 1780, he moved to the 64-gun *Belliqueux*. While commanding her, the ship participated in the battles of Fort Royal and the Chesapeake in 1781, then St Kitts, the Saintes, and the Mona Passage in 1782. Thereafter, he commanded the 74s *Alexander* in 1782-1783 and *Powerful* in 1783-1786. On the Retired List, he was promoted to Rear-Admiral in 1790 and Vice-Admiral in 1794. He died on 13 September 1794 at Stoke Damerel, Plymouth.

108 **Captain George Ourry** commanded *Somerset* from 1776 to 1778. Born in the Channel Islands in 1732 the grandson of a Huguenot refugee, he was the youngest of four brothers. Three served in the Royal Navy and one in the Army. George Ourry joined the Navy 20 October 1746. He passed his Lieutenant's Examination on 2 July 1755 and was commissioned a Lieutenant one week later on 9 July 1755. He first served in the East Indies, where he was promoted to Commander on 24 August 1761 and placed in command of the 28-gun storeship *Southsea Castle* in 1761-1762. During the operations connected with the capture of Manila, he served as acting Captain of the 60-gun *Panther* and led a battalion of seamen ashore. He was promoted to Captain and placed in command of the 74-gun *Norfolk* on 10 November 1762 until 29 July 1764.

St. Alban's,	64	500	Captain Onslow.[109]
Ardent,	64	500	Captain Keppel.[110]

---

109 **Captain Richard Onslow** commanded *St Albans* from 31 October 1776 to February 1780. The younger son of Lieutenant-General Richard Onslow (c. 1697-1760) and nephew of the Speaker of the House of Commons, Arthur Onslow (1691-1768), Richard Onslow was born on 23 June 1741. He was commissioned a Lieutenant in the Royal Navy on 17 December 1758, then promoted to Commander on 11 February 1761 in command of the new 14-gun sloop *Martin*. He was promoted to Captain on 14 April 1762, commanding the 44-gun *Humber*. While escorting a convoy in the North Sea the ship wrecked on the Haysborough Sands off the coast of Norfolk on 14 April 1762. A court martial acquitted Onslow, placing the blame on the pilot. On 29 November 1762, he took command of the 44-gun *Phoenix* in the Mediterranean until she was paid off on 22 May 1763. He returned to sea duty in January 1766 to command the 28-gun frigate *Aquilon* until 1769. Subsequently, he commanded the 32-gun *Diana* in 1770-1773, then briefly the 60-gun *Achilles* for three months in 1773. He was unemployed until taking command of *St Albans* in 1776. In her, he participated in the defense of New York. After the Rhode Island operation, his ship went aground on Cape Cod, but got off. Afterwards, she participated in the Battle of St Lucia before returning to England, where the ship was found to be in poor condition and paid off. Onslow and his men transferred to the 74-gun *Bellona*, which Onslow commanded in 1780-1783. He subsequently commanded the 74s, *Triumph* in 1787-1789 and *Magnificent* in 1789-1791. He was promoted to Rear-Admiral on 1 February 1793, then to Vice-Admiral on 4 July 1794. In 1796, he was appointed second in command to Admiral Duncan and commanded the rear at the Battle of Camperdown. In 1797, he was made 1st Baronet of Althain. He remained second in command in the North Sea until 1799, when he was promoted to Admiral and retired. In 1814, he was appointed Lieutenant-General of Marines and, in 1815, Knight Grand Cross of the Order of the Bath. He died on 27 December 1817 at Southampton.

110 **Captain George Keppel** commanded *Ardent* as the flagship for Rear-Admiral James Gambier from January 1778 until he returned to England with the ship in January 1779. The illegitimate son of the Earl of Albemarle, George Keppel was commissioned a Lieutenant on 14 May 1774 and promoted to Commander on 18 March 1777 while in command of the 14-gun ship sloop *Swift* which he had commissioned in January. He sailed in her for New York on 27 March 1777. He was promoted to Captain on 26 January 1778 in command of *Ardent*. Following the Rhode Island operation, the ship remained Gambier's flagship while in temporary command of the North American Station, and thereafter attached to Byron's Squadron. On 18 September 1778, Keppel exchanged posts with Captain Samuel Clayton to command the 28-gun frigate *Iris* (ex-Continental frigate *Hancock*). Returning to England in her, he commissioned the new 28-gun *Vestal* in November 1779, then sailed for Newfoundland in April 1780. With the sloop *Fairy*, he captured the American packet *Mercury*, carrying Henry Laurens, the returning American ambassador to The Dutch Republic, with a draft treaty between the United States and the Dutch. With this incident, Britain declared war and began the Fourth Anglo-Dutch War. Henry Laurens was declared a traitor and sent to the Tower of London. In 1780, Keppel took command of the 32-gun *Aeolus* in which he returned to Newfoundland. Then, on 1 January, he shifted to the command of the 74-gun *Fortitude*, operating in the North Sea and the in the relief of Gibraltar in 1782. On 4 December 1782 , he took command of the recently built and newly captured French prize, the 38-gun frigate *Hebe*. He remained in her until 16 April 1783, when his uncle, the First Lord of the Admiralty Admiral Augustus Viscount Keppel, removed him. Following this he fled to France because of his financial difficulties. After the outbreak of the French Revolution, he returned to Britain and was given command on 1 August 1794 of the 74-gun *Defiance*. He retained command of her until promoted to Rear-Admiral on 1 June 1794. By seniority, he was promoted to Vice-Admiral on 14 February 1799 and Admiral on 23 April 1804 before his death later that same year.

FOURTH RATE

Centurion,	50	350	Captain Brathwaite.[111]
Experiment,	50	320	Captain Sir James Wallace.[112]
Isis,	50	350	Captain Raynor.

---

[111] **Captain Richard Braithwaite** (or Brathwaite) commanded the newly commissioned *Centurion* from 14 July 1775 to 9 January 1781. Born to an influential family in Appleby, Westmoreland about 1728, he joined the Royal Navy on 30 June 1742. He was a considerably older first cousin to Cuthbert Collingwood. After serving as Master's Mate in the 44-gun *Humber* in 1752-54, he took his Lieutenant's Examination on 16 January 1754 and was commissioned a Lieutenant on 7 May 1755. Promoted to Commander on 29 November 1756, he commanded the 12-gun *Polacre* under Admiral Lord Hawke until 1760. He then commanded the 14-gun *Saltash* until he was promoted to Captain on 6 April 1761 and given command of the 28-gun frigate *Shannon*. He was unemployed from 1763 to 1766, when he took command of the 24-gun *Gibraltar*, then the 28-gun *Liverpool* in 1767-1772 and then *Milford* for a month in 1775 before moving to *Centurion*. In her, he participated in the landings on Staten Island in 1776, the occupation of Newport as Howe's flagship in December 1776, then at St Lucia in 1778 and Martinique in 1780. Moving to the 64-gun *Bienfaisant* in January 1781, he participated in the 1781 relief of Gibraltar and at the Battle of Dogger Bank on 5 August 1781. On the Retired List he was promoted to Rear-Admiral on 21 September 1790 and then to Vice-Admiral on 1 February 1793, and to Admiral on 14 February 1799. He died at Greenwich on 28 June 1805.

[112] **Captain Sir James Wallace** commanded *Experiment* from 4 June 1776 to 24 September 1779. He is more widely remembered in Rhode Island for his previous command, the 20-gun frigate *Rose*, from 15 November 1771 to 4 June 1776. Wallace was born in Lodden, Norfolk, in 1731. In 1746, he enrolled at the Royal Naval Academy in Portsmouth, where he studied until 22 August 1748. After serving in the 24-gun *Syren*, the 64-gun *Vigilant*, and *Intrepid*, he passed his Lieutenant's Examination on 3 January 1753. Commissioned a Lieutenant on 3 January 1755, he was assigned to the 50-gun *Greenwich*. Wallace was among the ship's company when the French 74-gun *La Diadème* and 64-gun *L'Eveillé* captured *Greenwich* off Cape Cabrón on the northeast coast of Santo Domingo (present-day Dominican Republic). After being released, he joined the 60-gun *Rippon* and then the 90-gun *Neptune*. He was promoted to Commander on 3 November 1762 to command the 10-gun *Alderney*. He went from her to command the 10-gun *Trial* in 1763-1766, and then *Bonetta* in 1767-1771. Promoted to Captain on 10 January 1771, he commanded the 28-gun *Unicorn* for eleven months before taking command of *Rose*. While in command of *Rose*, he took harsh measures in attempting to enforce the British Navigation Acts in and around Narragansett Bay, earning him much local enmity. On 25 June 1776, he exchanged posts with Captain Alexander Scott, who had lost an arm in action, and took command of the 50-gun *Experiment* and participated in the New York campaign in July-August 1776, then was present at the occupation of Newport in December 1776. He returned to England in January 1777 with dispatches, where he was appointed Knight Bachelor for his services in America. In July, he returned to New York, where he participated in attacking American forts on the Hudson River. On 20 August 1778, he was on detached duty off Newport, when d'Estaing's fleet arrived. Escaping to the West, Wallace sailed down Long Island Sound and, in a feat of seamanship not previously accomplished by such a large vessel, he took his ship through Hell Gate and into the East River to reach New York City on 25 August. In September, he captured the American 32-gun *Raleigh* off Penobscot, then, in December, a gale off the Chesapeake Capes forced *Experiment* back to England. Operating in the Channel, he participated in repulsing the French attack on Jersey in the English Channel in May 1779. He returned to North America, where the French captured his ship in September 1779. After a prisoner of war exchange, he returned to England in February 1780, where a court martial cleared him of blame for the loss of *Experiment*. He was ordered to the command of the 64-gun *Nonsuch* in which he captured the well-known 32-gun French frigate *Belle Poule*. Subsequently, he was with Darby's fleet at the relief of Gibraltar in 1781. In October 1781, he took command of the newly commissioned 74-gun *Warrior*, in which he participated in the Battle of the Saintes on 12 April 1782, and in the following week, the Battle of Mona Passage. He subsequently commanded the 74-gun *Resolution* from July to November 1782. Unemployed until 1790, he commanded the 74s *Swiftsure* in 1790-1791 and *Monarch* in 1792-1793. Promoted to Rear-Admiral in 1794 and Vice-Admiral in 1795, he served as commander-in-chief in Newfoundland. He hauled down his flag in 1796. In retirement, he lived at Hanworth House, Middlesex, and was promoted to Admiral in 1799. He died on 6 Match 1803.

Renown,	50	350	Captain Dawson (acting.)[113]

---

113 **Captain George Dawson** was appointed acting commanding officer of *Renown* on 9 June 1777 as a Commander, following the death of Captain Francis Banks. He was promoted to Captain on 9 September, but still commanding *Renown* in an acting capacity. He was given full command on 23 November 1779 and remained in her until 6 December 1780. Dawson was born about 1739 and first joined the Royal Navy on 22 June 1755. He passed his Lieutenant's Examination on 1 July 1761 and was commissioned Lieutenant on 9 August 1762. He commanded the 6-gun *Hope* from 1768 to 1771, and then the newly built 14-gun brig *Hope* from December 1775. Promoted to Commander on 13 May 1776, he remained in *Hope* until he ordered as acting Captain of *Renown*. On 1 August 1780, he exchanged posts with Captain James Hawker and took command of the 28-gun *Iris* (ex-Continental frigate *Hancock*) and participated in the Battle of Cape Henry on 16 March 1781. He captured the 32-gun Continental frigate *Trumbull* on 8 August 1780. The Comte de Barras's squadron captured him and his ship along with *Richmond*, in Chesapeake Bay on 11 September 1781. He was unemployed until 26 August 1786, when he took command of the 38-gun *Phaeton*. While operating in the Mediterranean, the sailing master of the ship brought 15-counts of tyranny, malversation, oppression, suttling, etc. A court marital proved two of the charges and he was dismissed from the service on 20 November 1788. In 1796, the Privy Council denied his for restoration of his rank.

FIFTH RATE

Phoenix,	44	280	Captain Parker.[114]
Roebuck,	44	280	Captain Hamond.[115]

---

114 **Captain Hyde Parker** took command of *Phoenix* on 4 June 1775 and remained in command until 4 October 1780. The second son of Vice-Admiral Sir Hyde Parker (1714-1783), 5th Baronet of Melford Hall, he was born in 1739. He first went to sea in November 1751 in his father's ship, the 70-gun *Vanguard*. He followed his father to commission the newly built 8-gun sloop *Cruizer*. In 1755, he transferred to the 60-gun *Medway*. He passed his Lieutenant's Examination on 7 November 1757 then commissioned Lieutenant on 25 January 1758. He served successively under his father in the 36-gun frigate *Brilliant*, the 68-gun *Grafton*, and then 74-gun *Norfolk*, participating in the reduction of Pondicherry and Manila. Thereafter, he transferred to the 74-gun *Lennox* in 1762. Promoted to Commander on 16 December 1762, he commanded the 14-gun *Manila* until he was promoted to Captain on 18 July 1763. He commanded the 20-gun *Baleine* in the East Indies in 1763-64, the 28-gun *Hussar* in North America in 1766-69, and then the 32-gun *Boston* in 1770-1772. On 21 April 1779, he was appointed Knight Bachelor for his command of *Phoenix*. He returned to the West Indies in *Phoenix* where the ship was driven ashore at Cap Cruz, Cuba, during a hurricane on 4 October 1780. Parker saved most of the 200-man crew and was able to return safely with them to Montego Bay, Jamaica, eleven days after the wreck. Cleared by a court-martial for the loss of the ship, he returned to England where he took command of the 38-gun *Latona*. He commanded the new 74-gun *Goliath* in 1781-1786, *Orion* 1787-88, and the yacht *Royal Charlotte* in 1788-1791. He promoted to Rear-Admiral in 1793 and Vice-Admiral on 4 July 1794, while serving in the Mediterranean. From 1796 to 1800, he served as Commander-in-Chief, Jamaica, being promoted to Admiral during that period on 14 February 1799. Returning to England, he was second in command in the Channel, then in 1801, he was appointed to command an expedition to the Baltic with Vice-Admiral Lord Nelson as his second in command. He was recalled after Nelson criticized him and did not serve again. He died on 16 March 1807.

115 **Captain Andrew Snape Hamond** commanded *Roebuck* from 4 July 1775 to 2 July 1781. He was born on 17 December 1738 at Blackheath, London, the son of a merchant and ship-owner. He entered the Navy in 1753 and passed his Lieutenant's Examination on 6 September 1758. Commissioned Lieutenant on 18 June 1759, he served in the 64-gun *Magnanime*, commanded by Captain Lord Howe, participating in the Battle of Quiberon Bay on 9 November 1759. He went on to command the 6-gun cutter *Grace* in the Solent during 1763-1764. Promoted to Commander on 20 June 1765, he briefly commanded the 18-gun *Merlin*, before commanding the 8-gun sloop *Savage* from 1766 to 1769. Promoted to Captain on 7 December 1770, he commanded the 90-gun *Barfleur* until 25 May 1771, then took command of the 32-gun *Arethusa* until 29 November 1773. He was appointed Knight Bachelor on 15 May 1779, recognizing his services in *Roebuck* in 1778 at Sandy Hook and Rhode Island. In May 1780, *Roebuck* served as flagship for Vice-Admiral Arbuthnot during the reduction of Charleston. On completion of the operation, Arbuthnot sent Hamond home with dispatches. In October 1780, he was appointed Lieutenant-Governor of Nova Scotia, Resident Commissioner at Halifax, and Commander-in-Chief. He resigned his civil role as Lieutenant-Governor in 1782 but retained his naval responsibilities until January 1783. On 10 December 1783, he was created 1st Baronet of Holly Grove. He served as Commander-in-Chief, River Medway and the Nore in 1785-1788, commanding the 74-gun *Irresistible*, following which he commanded *Vanguard* in 1790-1791, *Bedford* in 1791-1792 during which time he sat on the court-martial board of the *Bounty* mutineers, and then commanded 98-gun *Duke* in 1793-1794. He served as Comptroller of the Navy from 25 September 1794 until 3 March 1806. He was also Member of Parliament for Ipswich from 1796 to 1806. He died at his estate near Lynn, Norfolk, on 12 October 1828.

Venus,	36	240	Captain Williams.[116]
Richmond,	32	220	Captain Gidoin.[117]

---

116 **Captain William Peere Williams** commanded *Venus* from 10 March 1777 to 18 September 1778. Born on 6 January 1742 at the Episcopal Palace at Peterborough, where his father, the Rev'd Dr. Frederick Williams, was a prebendary of the Cathedral and his mother was the daughter of the Right Rev'd Robert Clavering, Bishop of Peterborough. He was the namesake of his paternal grandfather, a Member of Parliament for Bishop's Castle in Shropshire. He attended school at Stamford, then Eton, before entering the Royal Naval Academy at Portsmouth in 1757, while his name was carried on the books of *Royal Sovereign*. He first went to sea in 1759-1762 as a Midshipman in *Magnanime*, commanded by Captain Lord Howe. He was present at the Battle of Quiberon Bay, then followed Howe to the 80-gun *Princess Amelia*, while Howe was flag captain to Rear-Admiral Prince Edward, Duke of York and Albany in 1762-1763, then joined the 50-gun *Romney* on the North American Station. Promoted to Lieutenant on 18 September 1764, he moved to the 44-gun *Rainbow* until 1766. Promoted to Commander on 26 May 1768, he commanded the bomb-ketch *Thunder* until 1771. He was promoted to Captain on 10 January 1771 and successively commanded the 30-gun *Renown* in 1771, the 28-gun *Active* in 1771-1773, and the 20-gun *Lively* until the end of 1773. He returned home in poor health after service in the West Indies and Newfoundland, but had recovered by early 1777, when he took command of *Venus*. On 18 August 1778, he exchanged posts with Captain James Ferguson to take command of the 32-gun *Brune* to take the Peace Commissioners back to England, where the ship was paid off. On Half Pay in 1779, he took command of the new 36-gun *Flora* on 13 April 1780 and remained in command until 15 November 1781, during which period he was in several actions. Not employed again, he was promoted in retirement to Rear-Admiral in 1794, to Vice-Admiral in 1795, to Admiral in 1799, and Admiral of the Fleet in 1830. He inherited three valuable properties. In 1821, he took the additional surname of Freeman, when he inherited the state of Fawley Court near Henley-on-Thames. He died at Yew House, Hoddesdon, his estate in Hertfordshire, on 11 February 1832.

117 **Captain John Lewis Gidoin** commanded *Richmond* from 13 March 1776 to 22 July 1777. Gidoin was born about 1727 and joined the Navy on 28 June 1742. He passed his Lieutenant's Examination on 11 October 1748 and was promoted to Lieutenant more than five years later, 19 January 1755. He was promoted to Commander on 9 March 1759 while commanding the 12-gun storeship *Port Royal*. On his promotion, he moved to command the 12-gun storeship *Port Antonio* at Jamaica from 20 March 1759 until 22 July 1761, when he was ordered to bring the 28-gun *Valeur* home to Deptford from Jamaica. He then commanded the 10-gun *Zephyr* from 3 May 1762 to 15 July 1763, in which she operated off the coast of Portugal. On 15 July 1763, he commissioned the new 10-gun *Jamaica* and sailed for New England, where she operated until coming home to be being paid off 11 February 1767. He was promoted to Captain on 26 May 1768 but did not go to sea. He commanded the Impress Service at Falmouth in 1770-1771, then in 1776, recommissioned the newly copper-sheathed *Richmond*. The ship returned from America in April 1779. He then commanded a squadron that included Sir James Wallace's *Experiment* to repulse the French designs on Jersey at Cancale Bay in May 1779. On Half Pay from July to December 1779, Gidoin took command of the 74-gun *Torbay* on Christmas Day 1779 in which he sailed to the West Indies and participated in the occupation of St Eustatius in February 1781, the Battle of Fort Royal, Martinique on 17 April 1781, the Battle of St Kitts 25-26 January 1782, and the Battle of the Saintes 12 April 1782. He left *Torbay* on 17 March 1783 in the West Indies and returned home but was not employed again. In retirement, he was promoted to Rear-Admiral on 12 April 1794 and to Vice-Admiral on 1 June 1795. He died in February 1796 at Modbury, Devon.

Pearl,	32	220	Captain Linzee.[118]
Apollo,	32	220	Captain Pownoll.[119]

---

118 **Captain John Linzee** commanded *Pearl* from 21 May 1777 until 9 January 1779. Linzee was born on 25 March 1743. He was a cousin of Susannah Linzee, wife of the future Admiral Samuel Lord Hood. Linzee was serving in the 50-gun *Romney*, flying the broad pennant of Captain Samuel Hood, commanding the North American Station, when he was commissioned Lieutenant on 13 October 1768. He was immediately given temporary command of the 6-gun schooner *Halifax*. In May 1769, he rejoined Hood in *Romney* and soon became the ship's first lieutenant. In October 1770, he was given command of the 14-gun ship sloop *Beaver* engaged in anti-smuggling operations on the Rhode Island coast . He was promoted to Commander and confirmed in his command on 19 January 1771. He became deeply involved in the aftermath of the *Gaspee* affair while he also courted and married Susannah Inman, daughter of a Loyalist from Cambridge, Massachusetts. He returned to England with his American wife and left command of *Beaver* on 28 October 1772. Two years passed before he took command on 13 October 1774 of the 14-gun sloop *Falcon* in which he returned to New England. In June 1775, he supported British forces during the Battle of Bunker Hill and in August fourteen of his men were captured during his unsuccessful operations off Cape Ann. He retained command of *Falcon* until promoted to Captain on 16 February 1777. After some disagreement between Linzee's seniors over his assignment, Linzee took command of *Pearl*. Shortly after the Rhode Island operation, he sailed to the Leeward Islands, where he exchanged posts with Captain Alexander Graeme and took command of the 32-gun *Diamond* 9 January 1779. While returning to Britain in September, he shared in capturing two French merchant ships, then was sent on an unsuccessful mission to chase Captain John Paul Jones during his attacks on British shipping in northern England and Scotland. On Half Pay from November 1779, he was given command on 17 August 1780 of the 36-gun captured Spanish frigate *Santa Monica*. In her he returned to the West Indies, where he served again under Rear-Admiral Samuel Hood. He was with Hood at Martinique, St Lucia, and later at the Battle of the Chesapeake Capes. After a mutiny, the ship ran aground on an uncharted rock and sank off Tortola in the Virgin Islands. After six years of unemployment, Linzee took command of the 32-gun *Penelope* in December 1788, serving in her in the Leeward Islands and Nova Scotia until November 1790. Linzee resigned from the Navy following the death of his wife in 1792 and retired to Milton, Massachusetts, where he died on 8 October 1798.

119 **Captain Philemon Pownoll** commanded *Apollo* from 1 January 1777 to 16 June 1780. Born about 1734, the son of Israel Pownall, the master-shipwright at Plymouth Dockyard, he joined the Royal Navy on 20 March 1751 and passed his Lieutenant's Examination on 9 April 1755. Promoted to Lieutenant on 7 October 1755 and then to Commander on 6 August 1759, he commanded the 16-gun ship sloop *Favorite* until 6 August 1762. While commanding her, his ship was present when Captain Charles Proby's squadron captured two French frigates and a 64-gun warship in July 1761. Then, on 21 May 1762, with the frigate *Milford*, he captured the Spanish merchant ship *Hermione*, carrying a rich cargo from Peru to Cadiz. The most valuable capture made during the Seven Years' War, Pownoll's share of the prize money was a massive £64,872, or some 640 times his annual naval pay. On leaving *Favorite*, he was unemployed. Promoted to Captain on 10 January 1771, it was almost four years before he had an active sea command. On 4 December 1775, he took command of the 32-gun *Blonde* for two years, then took command of *Apollo*. One of Pownoll's young protégés in both ships was the future Admiral Edward Pellew, Viscount Exmouth. A popular and successful officer, Pownall fought several successful frigate actions and was killed in action on 15 June 1780.

SIXTH RATE

Sphynx,	20	160	Captain Graeme.[120]
Sloop *Nautilus,*	16 Guns,	125 Men,	Capt. Becher.[121]
Armed Ship *Vigilant,*	20 Guns,	150 Men,	Captain Christian.[122]

120 **Captain Alexander Graeme** commanded *Sphinx* from 24 January 1778 to 24 November 1778. Graeme was born on 9 December 1741 at Graemeshall, Holm, Orkney Islands. He was commissioned a Lieutenant on 17 December 1760 and served in the 68-gun *Temple* and the 28-gun *Aquilon* in the Leeward Islands. With the end of the Seven Years' War, he went on to Half Pay in September 1763. A year later, he was back serving on guardships at Portsmouth, then on 17 October 1765, he took command of the 10-gun schooner *Egmont* and saw service in Newfoundland in 1767 and off the Irish coast before leaving the ship on 2 February 1771. He was unemployed until 26 January 1774, when he became the second Lieutenant in the 50-gun *Preston*, flagship of Vice-Admiral Samuel Graves on the North American Station. Promoted to Commander on 15 November 1775, he commanded the 14-gun ship sloop *Kingfisher* until 14 January 1778. He participated in the December 1776 occupation of Newport and in 1777 was stationed in Narragansett Bay's Sakonnet Passage before staking command of *Sphinx*. In November 1778, he moved to command the 32-gun frigate *Diamond* and sailed for Barbados. He exchanged posts with Captain John Linzee on 9 January 1779 and took command of *Pearl*, bringing her home to pay off 13 April 1779. On Half Pay until 14 July, when he took command of the 14-gun *Tartar* in which he captured the 28-gun Spanish frigate *Santa Margarita* in November 1779 and *Infanta Carlotta* in 1780. On 13 February 1781, he left *Tartar* to take command of the 50-gun *Preston* on 13 March. He fought in the Battle of Dogger Bank on 5 August 1781, in which he lost an arm. Leaving command on 13 August, he went off Half Pay for thirteen years and inherited family estates. On 5 January 1795, he returned to sea duty to command the 98-gun *Glory* for six months before being promoted to Rear-Admiral on 1 June 1795. He was promoted to Vice-Admiral on 14 February 1799 and a few months later was appointed commander-in-chef at the Nore, serving in that position until 1803. In retirement, he was promoted to Admiral on 23 April 1804. He died on 5 August 1818 in Edinburgh.

121 **Captain [Commander] John Becher** commanded *Nautilus* from 1 February 1778 to 3 April 1779. Born in London in 1726, he was commissioned a Lieutenant on 21 January 1757 and promoted to Commander on 1 February 1778. He had no other known service and died in 1784.

122 **Captain [Commander] Brabazon Christian** commanded *Vigilant* from 22 November 1777 to 12 December 1779. Born in Ireland in 1755, he was commissioned a Lieutenant on 18 July 1776. He was promoted to Commander on the day he took command of *Vigilant*. In 1779, he participated in siege of Savannah. On 1 January 1780, he was promoted to Captain in command of the 20-gun frigate *Seaford*, escorting conveys in the Channel and in the Irish Sea. Remaining in command until 3 December 1781. On 24 December 1781, he took command of the 28-gun *Cyclops*. Initially operating in the North Sea, he sailed to North America in April 1782, where he took two French ships in 1783. On 19 September 1784, he moved to command the 20-gun *Daphne* until 25 December 1787. He died in 1789 at Balynakill, County Waterford, Ireland.

Fireship *Strombolo*,	45 Men,	Captain Aplin.[123]
Ditto *Sulphur*,	45 Men,	Captain Watt.[124]
Ditto, *Volcano*,	45 Men,	Captain O'Hara.[125]

---

123 Captain [Commander] Peter Alpin commanded *Strombolo* 23 April 1778 to 16 April 1779. One of many children of Benjamin Alpin, an Oxfordshire lawyer, he was born in 1753 and joined the Navy on 26 May 1764 as a captain's servant in the yacht *William and Mary*. Subsequently he served in the 50-gun *Guernsey* and then the sloop *Savage* under Captain Andrew Snape Hamond in 1769-1770. He joined *Niger* in the Mediterranean in 1770-1772 and *Prudent* in the East Indies in 1772-1775. He passed his Lieutenant's Examination on 9 August 1775, then served in the 44-gun *Roebuck*, again under Hamond as a Midshipman, when he was commissioned a Lieutenant on 9 August 1776. He was appointed Third Lieutenant in *Roebuck* on 10 October 1776 and remained in this assignment until 23 April 1778, when he was promoted to Commander and took command of *Strombolo*. He left the fireship to take command of the 14-gun, brig-sloop *Swift* (ex-Connecticut privateer *Middletown*). He remained in her until promoted to Captain on 23 October 1780, when he took command of the 24-gun frigate *Fowey*. Operating in Chesapeake Bay, Aplin was forced to scuttle and burn the ship to prevent De Grasse's fleet from capturing her. Immediately afterward, he served ashore with General Cornwallis's Army until its surrender. He was not employed again for sixteen years until July 1797, when he took command of the 74-gun *Hector*. He remained in her until 1799, when he was promoted to Rear-Admiral and retired. He was subsequently promoted to Vice-Admiral on 9 November 1805, and to Admiral on 31 July 1810. He died on 17 April 1817 at Brickstone House near Cheltenham.

124 Captain [Commander] James Watt commanded *Sulphur* from 25 July 1778 to 29 September 1778. Born about 1733, he joined the Royal Navy on 5 April 1755 and passed his Lieutenant's Examination on 11 Aril 1759. Commissioned a Lieutenant on 24 June 1762, he served in the 32-gun frigate *Pearl* until 1766. Not employed again until 10 May 1776, he joined Vice-Admiral Lord Howe's flagship, *Eagle*, at New York serving as fifth lieutenant for a year until 11 May 1777. He served briefly as first lieutenant under Andrew Snape Hamond in the frigate *Roebuck*. During the Philadelphia campaign, Hamond placed him in command of the captured 28-gun Continental frigate *Delaware*. Howe promoted Watt to Commander on 11 November 1777 in command of *Delaware*, continuing until 22 April 1778. Then, on 25 July 1778 he took command of the newly purchased 8-gun fireship *Sulphur*, taking her back to England to be refitted. Promoted to Captain on 9 May 1781, he commanded the 74-gun *Sultan* in the East Indies, participating in the Battle of Providien on 12 April 1782 and the second battle of Negapatam on 6 July 1782. He was killed in action during the Battle of Trincomalee on 3 August 1782.

125 Captain [Commander} William O'Hara commissioned the recently-purchased *Volcano* on 31 July 1778 and remained in command until 15 February 1780. The vessel was the former merchant ship *Empress of Russia* that Lord Howe purchased in North America. William Henry King O'Hara is reputed to have been the illegitimate son of Field Marshal James O'Hara, 2nd Baron Tyrawley (1682-1774), and a brother of the illegitimate General Charles O'Hara (1740-1802), who had represented the British forces that surrendered to George Washington at Yorktown. William O'Hara was commissioned a Lieutenant on 16 January 1768. In 1773, he was serving as Third Lieutenant on board the 74-gun *Marlborough*. He was promoted to Commander on 31 January 1778. On relinquishing command of *Volcano*, he was posted Captain in command of the 20-gun *Scarborough* and sailed to the Leeward Islands and Jamaica. In September 1789, he replaced Captain Horatio Nelson, who had been appointed to command the 44-gun *Janus* but never took command due to an illness. O'Hara remained in her until 1783, when he moved to the 32-gun *Andromache*. After commanding her for three years in the Mediterranean, he transferred to command the 32-gun *Ambuscade* in 1787, also in the Mediterranean. He died while commanding *Ambuscade* in December 1789.

Bomb Vessel *Thunder*,	8 Guns,	80 Men,	Captain Gambier.[126]
Ditto *Carcass*,		70 Men,	Lieut. Edwards (acting.)[127]

---

126 **Captain [Commander] James Gambier** commanded *Thunder* from 9 March 1778 to 14 August 1778. Born on 13 October 1756 in the Bahamas, where his father John Gambier was serving as Lieutenant Governor, he had been sent home to be raised by his father's sister and her husband, Charles Middleton, the future Admiral Lord Barham. Another uncle was Rear-Admiral, later Vice-Admiral James Gambier (1723-1789), Commander-in-Chief on the North American station. The nephew had entered the Navy in 1767 and served under his uncle Captain (later Vice-Admiral) James Gambier on two successive ships. Commissioned Lieutenant on 12 February 1777, he was promoted to Commander to command *Thunder*. Promoted to Captain on 9 March 1778, he commanded the 32-gun *Raleigh* until 24 April 1781. He subsequently commanded the 44-gun *Endymion* in 1781-82. Then in 1793-94, he commanded the 74-gun *Defence*, earning distinction at the Battle of the Glorious First of June 1794. He was promoted to Rear-Admiral in 1795, to Vice-Admiral in 1799, to Admiral in 1810, and to Admiral of the Fleet in 1830. He served as a Lord Commissioner of the Admiralty 1795-1801, 1804-1806, and 1807-1808. In 1809, he commanded at the controversial Battle of Basque Roads. In addition, he was Commander-in-Chief, Newfoundland, in 1802-1804, led the attack that captured the Danish Navy at Copenhagen in 1807, and was the chief British peace commissioner at the Treaty of Ghent that ended the War of 1812. In retirement, he was active in Anglican evangelical church missionary societies and was one of the founders of Kenyon College in Gambier, Ohio, in 1824. He died on 19 April 1833 at Iver, Buckinghamshire.

127 **Lieutenant [Commander] Edward Edwards** was acting commanding officer of *Carcass* from 22 April 1778 until 17 June 1780. Born about 1723 in Water Newton, near Peterborough, he was the fifth of six children. He joined the Royal Navy on 30 April 1746. He passed his Lieutenant's Examination on 14 March 1755. Not being immediately promoted, he commanded the 24-gun privateer *Viscount Falmouth* from November 1757. Promoted to Lieutenant on 7 September 1759, he served as second Lieutenant in the 28-gun frigate *Active* in 1767 and, ten years later, was serving in the 64-gun *Augusta* on the North American Station in 1777. He was promoted to Commander on 22 April 1778 in command of *Carcass*. Shortly after the Rhode Island operation, he sailed for the Leeward Islands and participated in the defense of St Lucia in December 1778. On 17 June 1780, he took command of the 14-gun *Hornet* until he was promoted to Captain on 25 April 1781 and moved to the command of the new 20-gun *Narcissus*. While in her, he hung six of his men for mutiny and flogged fourteen others. After she was paid off in March 1784, he was not employed until he took command of the 24-gun *Pandora*, which had been refitted to search for and bring home the *Bounty* mutineers. On Tahiti in March and April 1791, he found fourteen of them and confined them on board *Pandora*. Not finding Fletcher Christian and the group that had gone to Pitcairn Island, he sailed for home with his prisoners. En route, the ship was wrecked in the Torres Strait on 28 August 1791. Four of the mutineers and 31 of the ship's crew drowned, but Edwards brought the survivors to Timor in an open boat. The surviving mutineers were confined on board a Dutch ship that brought Edwards and his men back to England. A court martial exonerated Edwards for the loss of *Pandora*. He was not employed at sea again but did serve as regulating officer responsible for discipline ashore in Argyllshire and Hull. In retirement, he was promoted by seniority to Rear-Admiral in 1799, Vice-Admiral in 1805, and Admiral in 1810. He died on 13 April 1815 at Stamford.

Galley *Philadelphia*,   Lieutenant Paterson.[128]
Ditto *Hussar*,   Lieutenant Sir James Barclay.[129]
Ditto, *Ferret*,   Lieutenant O'Brien.[130]

---

128 **Lieutenant Charles William Paterson** briefly commanded the armed galley *Philadelphia* in August 1778. Paterson was born in 1756 in Berwick-upon-Tweed, the son of James Peterson, a Captain in the 69th Regiment of Foot. On first going to sea in 1769, he served in 44-gun *Phoenix* under his uncle, Captain George Anthony Tonyn. Between 1772 and 1775, he served in the 32-gun *Flora* and the 20-gun *Rose*. As a Midshipman, he sailed for North America in February 1776 on board *Eagle*, Admiral Lord Howe's flagship on the North American Station. On 3 February 177, he was promoted to Lieutenant and served in the fireship *Strombolo* before moving to command *Philadelphia*. Following the Rhode Island operation, he was assigned to the 32-gun frigate *Brune*, in which he returned to England in 1779. Assigned in June 1779 as first lieutenant of the 64-gun *Ardent*, the Franco-Spanish fleet captured the ship off Torbay on 17 August 1779. On his release, he joined the 74-gun *Alcide* as she was sailing for the West Indies in May 1780. After participating in the capture of St Eustatius on 3 January 1781, he joined Rodney's flagship, *Sandwich*, then returned home in *Gibraltar*. He joined the new flagship for the Leeward Islands, the 90-gun *Formidable* and returned to that station in late 1781. In February 1782, he was appointed acting Captain of the armed ship *St. Eustatius*. On 8 April 1782, he was promoted to Commander in command of the 8-gun fireship *Blast* and participated in the blockade of Cape François and served at Jamaica, before going home to be paid off in April 1783. After a ten-year hiatus, Paterson took command of the store-ship *Gorgon* on 22 April 1793 and sailed for the Mediterranean. Remaining in her until he was promoted to Captain on 20 January 1794 and took command of the 20-gun *Ariadne*. He participated in the 1794 campaign at Corsica until he was given command of the captured French 38-gun *Melpomene* on 10 August 1794 to bring her home in early 1795. Thereafter followed five years of shore assignments. In 1799, he returned to sea duty as acting commanding officer of the 74-gun *Montagu*, then flag captain to Rear-Admiral John Knight. From January 1801 to May 1802, he commanded the 36-gun *San Fiorenzo*, taking a convoy to the Mediterranean and attending on the Royal Family at Weymouth. He was not reemployed until 1810, when he took command of Porchester Castle and its French prisoners of war at Portsmouth. In 1811-1812, he commanded the guard ship *Puissant* at Spithead. He retired in promotion to Rear-Admiral on 12 August 1812, to Vice-Admiral on 12 August 1819, and to Admiral 10 January 1837. He died on 10 March 1841 at East Cosham House, Hampshire.

129 **Lieutenant Sir James Barclay** commanded *Hussar* during the defense of New York and Rhode Island operations in August 1778. Born at Kingston, Hampshire, on 2 October 1750, he was the second son of Sir William Blois Barclay, 5th Baronet Barclay of Pierston, Ayrshire. He went to sea as a boy and was present at the capture of Havana in 1762. In 1769, he succeeded his brother as baronet. He passed his Lieutenant's Examination in 1770 and was commissioned a Lieutenant on 4 March 1777 and assigned to the 32-gun frigate *Amazon*. He was serving in the 100-gun *Britannia* with the Channel Fleet when he was promoted to Commander on 1 May 1782 and the command of the 18-gun ship sloop *Harpy*. He held command of *Harpy* as part of Lord Howe's fleet until the ship was paid off in March 1783, although he was promoted to Captain on 21 January 1783. After a gap of more than three years, he took command of the 62-gun *Leander* on 23 August 1786, during this period, *Leander* was the flagship for Commodore, then Rear-Admiral, Sir Herbert Sawyer in Nova Scotia, returning home in August 1788. From 6 July until October 1790, during the Spanish armament threat and Nootka Sound crisis, Barclay commanded the newly commissioned 98-gun *Windsor Castle*, flagship of Rear-Admiral Sawyer. He saw no further service and died at the Free Imperial City of Aix-La-Chapelle (Aachen), on 12 June 1793.

130 **Lieutenant John O'Bryen** commanded the armed galley *Ferret* during the Rhode Island campaign. He was commissioned a Lieutenant on 13 February 1777. In April 1783, he served briefly in the 64-gun *Ardent*, before becoming acting fourth lieutenant in the 90-gun *Queen*, remaining in her for three years until 22 April 1786. Promoted to Commander on 22 November 1790, he commanded the 44-gun frigate *Resistance*, temporarily refitted as a troop ship carrying 22 guns, while carrying troops to Gibraltar and to Canada. On 10 October 1793, he moved to command the 16-gun ship-sloop *Shark* and sailed to Newfoundland in 1795. He was promoted to Captain on 23 May 1797, retaining command of *Shark* into 1798. He was not employed further and died on 26 January 1804.

Ditto *Cornwallis*,   Lieutenant Spry.[131]

HOWE

Copy of a Letter from Captain Brisbane to the Viscount Howe, dated Flora off Newport, July 27, 1778.[132]

MY LORD,

I Have just now the Honor of your Lordship's Letter of the 19th Instant in Answer to mine of the 7th by the *Falcon*, since which I wrote you by the *Fowey* on the 19th: Also your Lordship's Orders to make War upon, take or destroy all Ships of the French Nation appearing on the Coast of North America; and have given Orders, in Consequence thereof, to the Captains and Commanders of the several Ships and Vessels under my Orders.

Major-General Sir Robert Pigot acquaints me, the Batteries on Goat Island, Brenton's Neck, Dumplins, and that at the North End of the Town, are put in the best State of Defence possible for the Time, in order to prevent any hostile Intention of the Enemy.

Agreable to your Lordship's Intimation respecting the Ships under my Orders, should the Enemy appear, and endeavor to get in, I shall take the best Precautions, according to Circumstances, for their Safety. I must observe to your Lordship, that Lieutenant Knowles,[133] agreeable to my Directions, has

---

131 **Lieutenant Thomas Spry** commanded the armed galley *Cornwallis* from 1 December 1777, the day he was commissioned a Lieutenant, and he remained in command until October 1778. From Cornwallis, he moved directly to the command of the 12-gun, New Bedford, Massachusetts, privateer *Greenwich* that the frigate *Maidstone* had captured in April 1778. On 21 May 1779, *Greenwich* ran aground in Stono Inlet, South Carolina, where on the following day, Spry burnt her to prevent her capture. He was not employed again for eight years, then took command of the 44-gun *Dover*, from October 1787 to January 1788. On 12 April 1813, he was designated a Superannuated Commander.

132 **Brisbane's letter to Howe** is transcribed in Michael J. Crawford., et al, eds., *Naval Documents of the American Revolution*, vol. 13 (2019), pp. 525-526, from The National Archives, Kew, ADM 1/488, fos. 321-22.

133 **Lieutenant John Knowles** served as the Agent for Transports at Newport, Rhode Island, from December 1776 to August 1778. Knowles was commissioned Lieutenant on 19 January 1759. He was promoted to Commander on 29 September 1778 and relieved Commander James Watt in command of the 8-gun fireship *Sulphur*, remaining in her only until 13 January 1779. Promoted to Captain on 1 July 1780, he commanded the 24-gun frigate *Fowey* for a year until 22 June 1781. He moved directly to commission the 50-gun Dutch prize *Rotterdam*, then sailed to North America, returned home, then sailed in her to the Leeward Islands. On 25 November 1782, he moved directly to command the 70-gun, Spanish prize *Diligent* as a guardship at Portsmouth until April 1783. He was not employed at sea again. He was promoted to Rear-Admiral on 14 February 1799. Of the 20 officers who had been agents for transports during the American War, he was one of only two men who were eventually promoted to flag rank.

got all the Transports and other Vessels into the inner Harbour, and placed the *Grand Duke* Storeship across the Mouth of the North Entrance, in order to prevent, as much as possible, the Enemy's destroying them: The *Pigot*, and Rebel Galley *Spitfire*,[134] are placed at the South Entrance to answer the same Purpose; and, in case the Enemy should come in, Lieutenant Knowles has Directions to scuttle the Transports.

As soon as I have Reason to apprehend the Enemy's Intention is not to attack this Port, I shall employ one of the advanced Ships with the *Sphynx* to convoy the Wood Vessels from Huntingdon[135] to this Port, and place the *Pigot* Galley in her Station.

As soon as I am joined by the Ship your Lordship intends assisting me with for the Protection of the Wood Vessels, I shall employ her in convoying such of them as the General may think proper to send to Fort-Pond Bay.[136]

In my present Situation I know no Mode of supplying the New Galley with Guns of the nearest Calibre she is constructed to bear, but by taking the 2 Eighteen-pounders out of the Rebel Galley *Spitfire*, which I propose doing if the Carriages will answer.

The Complements of the *Pigot* and *Spitfire* are nearly complete, and the Deficiencies shall be made up.

I have given the Surgeon of the *Flora* Directions to purchase Medicines for the Prisoners, agreeable to your Lordship's Directions on that Head; and have divided the Prisoners into Two Ships, separating those taken in Arms from the rest.

The 10 British Seamen brought from Boston are fit for Service; have been exchanged within the Limits of your Lordships former Directions, and distributed amongst the Ships, in order to complete Complements: But as I have already acquainted General Sullivan, that, agreeable to your Lordship's Orders, none of the New England Prisoners could be exchanged until Restitution was made for the

---

134 **The Rebel Galley *Spitfire*** is a reference to the Rhode Island Navy's schooner-rigged armed galley *Spitfire*, commanded by Joseph Crandall, that boats from the 64-gun *Nonsuch* had captured on 25 May 1778 while she was anchored off Fall River. Taken into the Royal Navy as a prize, she was commanded at this point by Lieutenant James Saumarez, the future famous Admiral and 1st Baron de Saumarez (1757-1836).

135 **Huntington** is located on the north shore of Long Island on Long Island Sound. Following the 1776 Battle of Long Island, British troops established an encampment there. Firewood for the use of the British garrison at Newport was often obtained from Huntington.

136 **Fort Pond Bay** is located off Long Island Sound near the western end of Long Island. The present-day town of Montauk, New York, is located on the bay.

Circumstance of the *Royal Bounty*;[137] and from a Rebel Colonel being very desirous to come to Newport to confer with General Pigot, he, as well as myself, have Reason to believe it has taken a proper Effect, from the Idea they are to be sent to England: The Conference will shew the Event.

Yesterday the *Sphynx* arrived from assisting in convoying the Vessels up the Sound: I intended to have sent her to cruize 10 or 12 Leagues to the Southward of Block Island, to prevent any Vessels bound to the Port of New York falling into the Enemy's Hands; but as Captain Harmood[138] acquaints me he has been informed by the People on Long Island that they have left the Hook, I shall order her to cruize between the Harbour's Mouth and Block Island, in order to give the earliest Intelligence.

As Lieutenant Andrew Congalton,[139] First Lieutenant of the *Flora*, still continues incapable of Duty, from the Wound he received some Time ago, I have given an Order to Mr. Smith, Master's Mate, to act as Second Lieutenant until his Recovery, or your Lordship's Pleasure is further known.

---

137 **Royal Bounty** was originally a ship that had been in the Greenland trade from Leith, Scotland. She had been captured in July 1777 near the Shetland Islands by the Massachusetts privateer *American Tartar*, then recaptured on 22 September by the frigate *Diamond* and her tender *Buckram*. She was sent into Halifax as a prize and sold on 13 December 1777. Captain Sir George Collier chartered her in Halifax, Nova Scotia, as a cartel ship, Thomas Compton, master, to be used for the exchange of prisoners under a flag of truce to Newport, Rhode Island. *Royal Bounty* had sailed from Halifax on 12 January 1778, carrying about 280 American prisoners, under the convoy escort of the brig *Cabot*. A few days after she sailed a gale separated the ship from her escort. When the American prisoners realized that *Cabot* was no longer in sight, they overpowered the crew of 15 men on 13-14 January and took the ship into Marblehead and held the ship there. British authorities were outraged that the Americans had broken the truce in taking the chartered ship.

138 **Captain [Commander] Harry Harmood** commanded the 14-gun sloop *Falcon* from 16 February 1777 to 5 August 1778, when she was sunk in Narragansett Bay to avoid capture. She was salvaged in November. Born at Salisbury in 1739, he entered the Royal Naval Academy at Portsmouth on 16 January 1752 and graduated in 1755. He was commissioned a Lieutenant on 19 February 1759 and assigned to the 28-gun *Aquilon*. By 1771, he was serving in the frigate *Arethusa* under Captain Andrew Snape Hamond on the North American Station, before being appointed Third Lieutenant in Howe's flagship, *Eagle*. While assigned to *Eagle*, he was promoted to Commander on 16 February 1777 and took command of *Falcon*. Nominally in command of *Falcon* until 17 October 1778, when he was promoted to Captain and the command of the 74-gun *Conqueror* flying the broad pennant of Commodore Thomas Graves. He sailed to the West Indies in December and was present at the Battle of Grenada on 6 July 1779. On 31 August 1779, he transferred to command the 98-gun *Princess Royal* in which he served until 5 June 1780, having participated in the Battle of Martinique in April 1780 and two fleet skirmishes in May. On 5 June 1780, he transferred to the 60-gun *Medway* and returned to England. While Medway was being refitted and coppered, Harmood temporary command of the 74-gun *Cumberland* in the Channel Fleet. Recommissioning *Medway* in January 1781, he participated in the relief of Gibraltar in April, the Channel Campaign during the summer and autumn, and the second battle of Ushant on 12 December 1781. He left *Medway* on 11 January 1782 and was not employed until March 1783, when he took command of the new 64-gun *Ardent* as guardship at Portsmouth, serving until 11 March 1786. He served as Extra Commissioner of the Navy Board from 25 September 1794 to 2 May 1795, then became Resident Commissioner at Sheerness Dockyard until 1801, when he moved to become Resident Commissioner at Chatham Dockyard. He was reappointed a Commissioner of the Navy from 3 August 1796 to 20 June 1806. He additionally served as Governor of Greenwich Hospital in 1806-1809. He died in London in February 1809.

139 **Lieutenant Andrew Congalton** had lost an arm while assisting the galley *Pigot*, which had gone aground within range of the American battery at Bristol Ferry on 30 May 1778. He had been commissioned a Lieutenant on 4 June 1777. After he served as first lieutenant in the frigate *Southampton* in 1786-1789. He was designated a Superannuated Commander on 27 August 1810 and died in 1823.

Captain Harmood's Orders from Admiral Gambier being to return immediately, I have therefore dispatched him, with Orders to return to his Station, and forward any Letter to your Lordship as soon as possible.

I am, with great Respect,

My Lord,

Your Lordship's most obedient humble Servant,

J. BRISBANE.

The London Gazette

Numb. 11921.

Publiſhed by Authority

From Saturday, October 24 to Tueſday, October 27, 1778

About the Facsimile

The London Gazette report of the Battle of Rhode Island presented in the transcription and annotations of the prior pages is identified in the facsimile by a solid black border. Readers will note that the full issue shows the broader context of the reporting of the battle, including such things as the September 1778 British attack by forces under the command of Major-General Charles Grey (1729-1807) on nearby Fairhaven, New Bedford, and Martha's Vineyard, Massachusetts.

At the end of Captain Brisbane's dispatch dated 27 July, the editor of the *Gazette* has added in an italicized note, marked by three asterisks, that states, *"There being no Possibility of Printing the Whole of Lord Howe's Dispatches To-night, the Remainder will be published in a Supplemental Gazette To-morrow."* However, as noted in the Introduction, no such supplemental issue of the Gazette is found on the official website, nor is there a continuation of Howe's dispatch in a later issue.

The facsimile is taken from the website of *The London Gazette*: The Gazette | Official Public Record: www.thegazette.co.uk.

From **Saturday** October 24, to **Tuesday** October 27, 1778.

Whitehall, October 27, 1778.

THE Difpatches, of which the following are Extracts, from General Sir Henry Clinton, Knight of the Bath, to the Right Honourable Lord George Germain, One of His Majefty's Principal Secretaries of State, were received on Sunday laft, from Lieutenant Grove, of His Majefty's Ship the Apollo, which left New York on the 17th of September, and arrived at Plymouth on the 23d Inftant.

New York, September 15, 1778.

I HAD the Honour of receiving your Lordfhip's Difpatches of the 12th of June and 1ft of July, by the Lord Hyde Pacquet, on the 18th of laft Month, and a Triplicate of your Letter N° 7, by the Lionefs, on the 7th Inftant.

I detached Major General Tryon, fome Time ago, to the Eaft End of Long Ifland, to fecure the Cattle on that Part; in which Situation he could either reinforce Rhode Ifland, or make a Defcent on Connecticut, as Circumftances might occur; and Tranfports for 4,000 Men were laying then in the Sound, and that Number of Troops ready for Embarkation on the fhorteft Notice.

In this State Things were, when Lord Howe failed for Rhode Ifland; and it was my Intention to proceed up the Sound, with the Troops above-mentioned, that they might be within his Lordfhip's Reach, in cafe we fhould fee an Opportunity for landing them to act with Advantage; but, on the 27th of laft Month, at the Inftant they were embarked, I received a Letter from Lord Howe, inclofing one from Major-General Pigot, by which I was informed, that the French Fleet had quitted Rhode Ifland; but that the Rebels were ftill there in great Force.

I thought it advifeable to fail immediately for the Relief of that Place, but contrary Winds detained us till the 31ft; and, on our Arrival, we found that the Enemy had evacuated the Ifland. For Particulars I muft beg Leave to refer your Lordfhip to Sir Robert Pigot's Letter, a Copy of which I have the Honour to inclofe. I was not without Hopes, that I fhould have been able to effect a Landing, in fuch Manner as to have made the Retreat of the Rebels from Rhode Ifland very precarious; or that an Opening would have offered for attacking Providence with Advantage: Being thwarted in both thefe Views by the Retreat of the Rebels, as the Wind was fair I proceeded towards New London, where I had Reafohto believe there were many Privateers; but the Wind coming unfavourable juft as I arrived off that Port, and continuing fo for Twenty-four Hours, I left the Fleet, directing Major-General Grey to proceed to Bedford, a noted Rendezvous for Privateers, &c. and in which there were a Number of captured Ships at that Time. For the Particulars of his Succefs, which has certainly been very complete, I muft beg Leave to refer your Lordfhip to the inclofed Letter.

I am, &c.
H. CLINTON.

Copy of a Letter from Major-General Pigot to General Sir Henry Clinton, dated Newport, Rhode Ifland, Auguft 31, 1778.

THough by my feveral Letters fince the 29th of July laft, more efpecially by that I had the Honour of writing by Lieutenant-Colonel Stuart, and the Accuracy of his Intelligence, your Excellency will have been informed of the State of Affairs here to the 28th Inftant; yet, as many of thofe Letters, from the Uncertainty of the Communication, may not have reached you, a Summary of the Tranfactions fince the 29th of July, when the French Fleet arrived, to the laft Period, will not be unneceffary, and may help to explain fubfequent Events.

From the firft Appearance of the Fleet to the 8th Inftant, our utmoft Exertions were directed to removing to Places of Security the Provifions, Ammunition, and Military and Naval Stores, which were either on board Ship, or on the Wharfs, preparing a fortified Camp, and difpofing every Thing for refifting the combined Attacks of the French and Rebels upon us; and I immediately withdrew from Conanicut Brown's Provincial Corps, and two Regiments of Anfpach, which had been ftationed there. The next Morning the Guns on the Beaver Tail and Dumplin Batteries; the former of which was directed with fome Effect againft two Line of Battle Ships that entered the Narraganzet Paffage, were rendered unferviceable, as the Fleet entering the Harbour would cut off all Communication with that Ifland; of which the French Admiral foon after took a temporary Poffeffion, and landed the Marines of his Squadron. During this Period, from the Movements of the French Ships in the Seaconet on the 30th, the King's Fifher and two Gallies were obliged to fet on Fire; and afterwards, on the 5th Inftant, the four advanced Frigates, from the Approach of two of the Enemy's Line of Battle Ships from the Narraganfet, were likewife deftroyed, after faving fome of their Stores, and fecuring the Landing of the Seamen.

When it was evident the French Fleet were coming into the Harbour, it became neceffary to collect our Forces, and withdraw the Troops from the North Parts of the Ifland, which was accordingly done that Evening. I likewife ordered all the Cattle on the Ifland to be drove within our Lines, leaving only one Cow with each Family, and every Carriage and Intrenching Tool to be fecured, as the only Meafures that could be devifed to diftrefs the Rebels and impede their Progrefs.

On the 8th Inftant, at Noon, the French Fleet (which from it's firft Appearance had continued with little Variation at Anchor about Three Miles from the Mouth of the Harbour) got under Way, and ftanding in under a light Sail, kept up a warm Fire on Brenton's Point, Goat Ifland, and the North Batteries, which were manned by Seamen of the deftroyed Frigates, and commanded by Captain Chriftian, Lieutenants Forreft and Otway of the Navy, who returned the Fire with great Spirit, and in a good Direction. The laft of thefe Works had been previoufly ftrengthened, and fome Tranfports funk in it's Front, as an effectual Meafure to block up the Paffage between it and Rofe Ifland.

The next Morning we had the Pleafure to fee the Englifh Fleet, and I immediately fent on Board to communicate to Lord Howe our Situation, and that of the Enemy. By Nine o'Clock the following Day the French Fleet repaffed our Batteries, and failed out of the Harbour, firing on them as before, and having it returned with equal Spirit on our Side. By this Cannonade from the Ships on both Days, very fortunately not One Man was hurt, or any Injury done, except to fome Houfes in Town.

I fhall now proceed to inform your Excellency of the

the Movements of the Enemy from the 9th Instant, when they landed at Howland's Ferry.

The Badness of the Weather for some Days must have prevented their transporting of Stores, or being in Readiness to approach us, as they did not make their Appearance near us 'till the 14th, when a large Body took Possession of Honyman's Hill.

To repel any Attempts from that Quarter, a Breastwork was directed to be made along the Heights from Green End to Irish's Redoubt, which was strengthened by an Abbatis.

On the 17th, the Enemy was discovered breaking Ground on Honyman's Hill, on the Summit of which, and on their Right of the Green End Road, they were constructing a Battery: The next Day another was commenced by them for Five Guns to their Left, and in a direct Line with the former, which was prepared for Four. On this Day a Line of Approach was likewise begun by them from the Battery on the Right to Green End Road, which Works we endeavoured to obstruct by keeping a continual Fire on them. The 19th the Enemy opened their Left Battery, which obliged our Encampment to be removed further in the Rear. This Day we began another Line, for the greater Security of our Left, from Irish's Redoubt to Pomini Hill; and I directed a Battery of 1 Twenty four and 2 Eighteen Pounders to be raised on our Right Breast Work to counteract those of the Enemy, which was opened the following Day, when they were observed busied in forming a second Approach from the first, to a nearer Distance on the Road.

At Noon the French Fleet again came in View, much disabled, and anchored off the Port, where it continued 'till the 22d, when it finally disappeared.

This Day the Rebels were constructing Two other Batteries much lower down the Hill than the former, one on the Right for Five, the other on the Left of Green End Road for Seven Guns, both which were opened the next Day, when I found it necessary to attempt silencing them, and therefore ordered a Battery for Seven heavy Guns, on commanding Ground, near Green End, which, from the Obstructions given by the Enemy's Fire, could not be completed 'till the 25th, when the Rebels thought proper to close the Embrasures of their lower Batteries, and make Use of them for Mortars. During this Time they had been constructing, on the Height of the East Road, another for One of Thirteen Inches; and this Day began a Third Approach in Front, and to the Right of their lower Batteries.

The 26th, observing the Enemy to discontinue their Works, and learning from Deserters, they were removing the Officers Baggage and Heavy Artillery, I detached Lieutenant Colonel Bruce, with a Hundred Men of the 54th Regiment, in the Night over Easton's Beach in Quest of Intelligence, who with great Address surprized and brought off a Piquet of Two Officers and Twenty-five Men, without any Loss. Some of Colonel Fanning's Corps, at different Times, exerted themselves in taking off People from the Enemy's advanced Posts; but little Intelligence to be depended upon was ever obtained from them; nor were other Attempts to procure it more efficacious, as from all that could be learned, it was doubtful whether their Intentions were to attack our Lines or retreat.

On the 27th the Sphynx and Two other Ships of War arrived; and I had the Honour of being informed by Colonel Stuart of your Excellency's Intention to reinforce this Post.

On the following Day the Vigilant Galley took a Station to cover the Left Flank of the Army; and at Ten o'Clock that Night the Rebels made an Attempt to surprize a Subaltern's Piquet from the Anspach Corps, but were repulsed, after killing One Man, and wounding Two others.

The 29th, at Break of Day, it was perceived that the Enemy had retreated during the night, upon which Major-General Prescott was ordered to detach a Regiment from the second Line under his Command, over Easton's Beach, towards the left Flank of the Enemy's Encampment, and a Part of Brown's

Corps was directed to take Possession of their Works. At the same Time Brigadier-General Smith was detached with the 22d and 43d Regiments, and the Flank Companies of the 38th and 54th, by the East Road. Major General Losberg marching by the West Road, with the Hessian Chasseurs and the Anspach Regiments of Voit and Seaboth, in order, if possible, to annoy them in their Retreat; and upon receiving a Report from General Smith, that the Rebels made a Stand, and were in Force upon Quaker's Hill, I ordered the 54th and Hessian Regiment of Huyn, with Part of Brown's Corps, to sustain him; but before they could arrive, the Perseverence of General Smith, and the spirited Behaviour of the Troops, had gained Possession of the strong Post on Quaker's Hill, and obliged the Enemy to retire to their Works at the North End of the Island. On hearing a smart Fire from the Chasseurs engaged on the West Road, I dispatched Colonel Fanning's Corps of Provincials to join General Losberg, who obliged the Rebels to quit two Redoubts made to cover their Retreat, drove them before him, and took Possession of Turkey Hill. Towards Evening, an Attempt being made by the Rebels to surround and cut off the Chasseurs, who were advanced on the Left, the Regiments of Fanning and Huyn were ordered up to their Support, and, after a smart Engagement with the Enemy, obliged them to retreat to their main Body on Windmill Hill.

To these Particulars I am in Justice obliged to add Brigadier-General Smith's Report, who, amidst the general Tribute due to the good Conduct of every Individual under his Command, has particularly distinguished Lieutenant-Colonel Campbell and the 22d Regiment, on whom, by their Position, the greater Weight of the Action fell. He also mentions with Applause the spirited Exertions of Lieutenant-Colonel Marsh and the 43d Regiment, of Captains Coore and Trench, who commanded the Flank Companies. He likewise acknowledges particular Obligations to all the Officers and Men of the Royal Artillery, as also to the Seamen who were attached to the Field Pieces; and has expressed his Thanks to Captain Barry, of the 52d Regiment, who was a Volunteer on this Occasion, and assisted in carrying his Orders. General Losberg has given his Testimony of the very good Behaviour of the Anspach Corps, commanded by Colonel de Voit, and of Captains Malsburg and Noltenius, with their Companies of Chasseurs.

After these Actions, the Enemy took Post in great Numbers on Windmill Hill, and employed themselves in strengthening that advantageous Situation.

This Night the Troops lay on their Arms on the Ground they had gained, and Directions were given for bringing up the Camp Equipage. Artillery were likewise sent for and Preparation made to remove the Rebels from their Redoubts; but by means of the great Number of Boats, they retreated in the Night of the 30th over Bristol and Howland's Ferry; thus relinquishing every Hold on the Island, and resigning to us its entire Possession.

During these tedious and fatiguing Operations, I was much indebted to the active Zeal of Captain Brisbane and all the Captains, other Officers and Men of the Navy, who enabled me to man the different Batteries with their most experienced Officers, and best Men, who by their Example and constant Attention contributed much in the Support of the Defences. And I must also take Notice of the good Inclination for the Service, shewn by the Marines of the different Ships, which occasioned my giving them in Charge the Defence of that principal Post on Fomini Hill. Nor can I conclude this Account, without expressing my sincere Acknowledgments to every Officer and Soldier under my Command, and to the several Departments, for their unwearied Exertions to counteract so many Difficulties.

The Prisoners taken on the 29th are not many in Number; but I have Reason to believe the Killed and Wounded of the Rebels is greater than that in the Return I have the Honor to inclose you of ours.

Return

Extract of a Letter from Major General Grey to His
Excellency Sir Henry Clinton, dated on board the
Carysfort Frigate off Bedford Harbour, Sep-
tember 6, 1778.

I AM happy to be able to acquaint you, that I have
been so fortunate, in the fullest Manner, to exe-
cate the Service your Goodness entrusted me with at
Bedford and Fair Haven.

A favorable Wind, and every possible Exertion
and Assistance received from the Navy, enabled us
to land so rapidly, Yesterday Evening about Six
o'Clock, that the Enemy had a very few Hours
Notice of our Approach: The Business was finished,
and the Troops all re-embarked this Morning by
Twelve o'Clock, with the Loss, which particularly
gives me Pleasure and Content, of only Five or Six
Men wounded, one of whom is since dead. The
Stores destroyed were valuable, and the Number of
Ships burnt about 70, Privateers and other Ships,
ready with their Cargoes in for failing. The only
Battery they had was on the Fair Haven Side, an
enclosed Fort with Eleven Pieces of Cannon,
which was abandoned, and the Cannon properly de-

molished by Captain Scott, Commanding Officer of
the Artillery, and the Magazine blown up.

I cannot enough praise the Spirit, Zeal and Acti-
vity of the Troops you have honored me with the
Command of upon this Service, also their Sobriety
in the Midst of Temptation, and Obedience to
Orders, as not one House in Bedford and Fair Haven, I think, was consumed that could be avoided,
except those with Stores.

I write in Haste, and not a little tired, therefore
must beg Leave to refer you for the late Plan o
Operations and Particulars to Captain Andre.

Extract of a Letter from General Sir Henry Clinton,
Knight of the Bath, to Lord George Germain
Dated New-York, Sept. 15, 1778.

IN Obedience to His Majesty's Commands signified
to me by your Lordship, every necessary Step
shall be taken by me, for the strict Observance of
what is stipulated in the Convention of Saratoga, on
the Part of Lieutenant-General Burgoyne, as well as
the fullest Assurance given, that the Troops when
embarked shall be sent to Great Britain, and every
Condition agreed upon between Lieutenant-General
Burgoyne and Major-General Gates, respecting them,
faithfully observed.

Extract of a Letter from General Sir Henry Clinton
to Lord George Germain, dated New York,
Sept. 21, 1778, brought by His Majesty's Ship
the Eagle, and received the 26th Instant.

IN my last I had the Honor to inform your Lordship of the Success of Major-General Grey at
Bedford and Fair-Haven. I have now the Pleasure
to transmit an Account of his whole Proceedings
upon that Expedition, which will shew how effec-
tually this Enterprize has been executed, and the
very great Loss the Enemy have sustained; at the
some Time that it reflects much Honor upon the
Abilities of the General, and the Behaviour of the
Troops employed on the Occasion.

Copy of a Letter from Major-General Grey to General Sir Henry Clinton, dated on Board the Carysfort, Whitestone, Sept. 18, 1778.

SIR,

IN the Evening of the 4th Instant, the Fleet, with
the Detachment under my Command, sailed from
New London, and stood to the Eastward with a very
favorable Wind. We were only retarded in the Run
from thence to Buzzard's Bay, by the altering our
course for some Hours in the Night, in consequence
of the Discovery of a strange Fleet, which was not
known to be Lord Howe's until Morning. By Five
o'Clock in the Afternoon of the 5th, the Ships were
at an Anchor in Clark's Cove, and the Boats having
been previously hoisted out, the Debarkation of the
Troops took place immediately. I proceeded without Loss of Time to destroy the Vessels and Stores,
in the whole Extent of Accushnet River (about six
Miles) particularly at Bedford and Fair-Haven, and
having dismantled and burnt a Fort on the East Side
of the River, mounting Eleven Pieces of heavy Cannon, with a Magazine and Barracks, completed the
Re-embarkation before Noon the next Day. I refer
Your Excellency to the annexed Return for the Enemy's Losses, as far as we were able to ascertain them,
and for our own Casualties.

The Wind did not admit of any further Move-
ment of the Fleet the 6th and 7th, than hauling a
little Distance from the Shore. Advantage was
taken of this Circumstance to burn a large Privateer
Ship on the Stocks, and to send a small Armament of Boats, with Two Galleys, to destroy two
or three Vessels, which being in the Stream, the
Troops had not been able to set Fire to.

From the Difficulties in passing out of Buzzard's
Bay into the Vineyard Sound, through Quickse's
Hole, and from Head Winds, the Fleet did not
reach Holme's Hole Harbour, in the Island of Martha's Vineyard, until the 10th. The Transports
with the Light Infantry, Grenadiers, and 33d Regiment, were anchored without the Harbour, as I
had

had at that Time a Service in View for thofe Corps, whilft the Bufinefs of collecting Cattle fhould be carrying on upon the Ifland. I was obliged by contrary Winds to relinquifh my Defigns.

On our Arrival off the Harbour, the Inhabitants fent Perfons on Board to afk my Intentions with refpect to them, to whom a Requifition was made of the Arms of the Militia, the Public Money, 300 Oxen, and 10,000 Sheep. They promifed each of thefe Articles fhould be delivered without Delay. I af.erwards found it neceffary to fend fmall Detachments into the Ifland, and detain the deputed Inhabitants for a Time, in order to accelerate their Compliance with the Demand.

The 12th I was able to embark on Board the Veffels, which arrived that Day from Rhode Ifland, 6000 Sheep, and 130 Oxen.

The 13th and 14th were employed in embarking Cattle and Sheep on Board our own Fleet; in deftroying fome Salt-Works; in burning or taking in the Inlets what Veffels and Boats could be found, and in receiving the Arms of the Militia. I here again refer your Excellency to Returns.

On the 15th the Fleet left Martha's Vineyard; and, after fuftaining, the next Day, a very fevere Gale of Wind, arrived the 17th at Whiteftone, without any material Damage.

I hold myfelf much obliged to the commanding Officers of Corps, and to the Troops in general, for the Alacrity with which every Service was performed.

I have the Honor to be, &c.
CHARLES GREY, M. G.

Return of Killed, Wounded and Miffing, of the Detachment under the Command of Major-General Grey.

1ft Battalion Light Infantry. 1 wounded, 3 miffing.
1ft Battalion of Grenadiers. 1 killed; 1 wounded; 3 miffing.
33d Regiment. 1 miffing.
42d Regiment. 1 wounded; 8 miffing.
46th Regiment. 1 miffing.
64th Regiment. 1 wounded.
Total. 1 killed. 4 wounded. 16 miffing.

The Enemy's Lofs, which came to our Knowledge, was an Officer and 3 Men killed by the advanced Parties of Light Infantry, who, on receiving a Fire from the Inclofures, rufhed on with their Bayonets. Sixteen were brought Prifoners from Bedford, to exchange for that Number miffing from the Troops.
(Signed) CHARLES GREY, M. G.

Return of Veffels and Stores deftroyed on Accufhnet River, the 5th of September, 1778.

8 Sail of large Veffels from 200 to 300 Tons, moft of them Prizes.
6 Armed Veffels carrying from 10 to 16 Guns.
A Number of Sloops and Schooners of inferior Size, amounting in all to 70, befides Whale-Boats and others: Amongft the Prizes were Three taken by Count d'Eftaing's Fleet.
26 Store-houfes at Bedford, feveral at M'Pherfon's Wharf, Crans Mills and Fair Haven: Thefe were filled with very great Quantities of Rum, Sugar, Melaffes, Coffee, Tobacco, Cotton, Tea, Medicines, Gunpowder, Sailcloth, Cordage, &c.
Two large Rope-walks.

At Falmouth in the Vineyard Sound, the 10th of September 1778.
2 Sloops and a Schooner taken by the Galleys, 1 loaded with Staves.
1 Sloop burnt.

In Old Town Harbour, Martha's Vineyard,
1 Brig of 150 Tons Burthen, burnt by the Scorpion.
1 Schooner of 70 Tons Burthen, burnt by ditto.
23 Whale Boats taken or deftroyed.
A Quantity of Plank taken.

At Holmes's Hole, Martha's Vineyard.
4 Veffels, with feveral Boats, taken or deftroyed.
A Salt Work deftroyed, and a confiderable Quantity of Salt taken.

Arms taken at Martha's Vineyard.
388 Stand, with Bayonets, Pouches, &c. fome Powder, and a Quantity of Lead, as by Artillery Return.

At the Battery near Fair Haven, and on Clark's Point.
13 Pieces of Iron Ordnance deftroyed, the Magazine blown up, and the Platforms, &c. and Barracks for 200 Men, burnt.
£ 1000 Sterling in Paper, the Amount of a Tax collected by Authority of the Congrefs, was received at Martha's Vineyard from the Collector.

Cattle and Sheep taken from Martha's Vineyard.
300 Oxen. 10,000 Sheep.
(Signed) CHARLES GREY, M. G.

Return of Ammunition, Arms and Accoutrements, &c. which were brought in by the Militia on the Ifland of Martha's Vineyard, agreeable to Major-General Grey's Order, received at Holmes's Cove, September 12, 13, and 14, 1778.

Tifbury. 132 Firelocks; 16 Bayonets; 44 Cartridge Boxes or Pouches; 11 Swords or Hangers; 22 Powder Horns.
Chilmark. 2 Halberts; 127 Firelocks; 20 Bayonets; 30 Cartridge Boxes or Pouches; 12 Swords or Hangers; 40 Powder Horns; 2 Piftols; 1 Drum.
Old Town. 129 Firelocks; 13 Bayonets; 3 Cartridge Boxes or Pouches; 2 Swords or Hangers; 9 Powder Horns, 2 Piftols.
Total. 2 Halberts; 388 Firelocks; 49 Bayonets; 77 Cartridge Boxes or Pouches; 25 Swords or Hangers; 71 Powder Horns; 4 Piftols; 1 Drum.
N. B. 1 Barrel, 1 Half Barrel, and 1 Quarter Barrel of Powder; a great Number of Lead Shot or Balls of different Sizes in Bags and Boxes; and a great many Flints.
(Signed) DAVID SCOTT, Captain Royal Reg. of Artillery.

Admiralty Office, October 27, 1778.
THE Difpatches from Vice-Admiral Lord Vifcount Howe, Commander in Chief of His Majefty's Ships in North America, to Mr. Stephens, of which the following are Extracts, were brought to this Office on Sunday laft by Lieutenant Grove, of His Majefty's Ship the Apollo, which Ship left New York the 17th of laft Month, and arrived at Plymouth the 22d Inftant.

Eagle, off Sandy Hook, Auguft 17, 1778.
IN Confequence of the Determination fignified in my Letter of the 31ft paft, and the Intelligence I had fubfequently received, that the French Squadron was feparated into different Detachments, ftationed off of the Entrance of the Middle Channel, and in the Narraganfet and Seaconet Paffages, for the Attack of Rhode Ifland, I attempted failing from Sandy Hook the 2d Inftant, with the Ships of War and attendant Veffels named in the annexed Lift, to profit by any Opportunity which might offer for taking Advantage of the Enemy in that divided Situation, and for the Relief, in that Cafe, of the Garrifon at Newport; but the Wind veering back to the Southward, and not afterwards correfponding fooner with the rifing of the Tide upon the Bar, my Departure was neceffarily poftponed until the Morning of the 6th; and I anchored the Squadron off of Point Judith the Evening of the 9th.

The Toulon Squadron had paffed the Batteries at the Entrance of the Harbour the preceding Day, and was moftly placed clofe over to the Conanicut Shore, in the middle Channel from Race Ifland Northward towards Dyers and Prudence Iflands.

Being thereby enabled to communicate immediately with the Garrifon, I was informed by Captain Brifbane

Brisbane of the Progress of the Enemy's Operations, together with the Destruction of the Frigates, and other Particulars since the Dates of his earlier Reports, as stated in the Copies of his several Letters herewith inclosed. By an Officer from the Major General Sir Robert Pigot I was at the same Time advised, that he had been obliged to evacuate Conanicut, as well as all his Out-posts on the Northern Parts of Rhode Island, and to confine his Defence to the Lines constructed on the Heights adjacent to the Town of Newport. Under these Circumstances I judged it was impracticable to afford the General any essential Relief.

The Wind changing to the North-East next Morning, the French Admiral stood out of the Port with the Twelve Two-decked Ships of his Squadron, named in the List transmitted with your Letter dated the 3d of May.

Deeming the Superiority of the Enemy's Force too great to come to Action with them, if it could be avoided, whilst they possessed the Weather-gage, I steered with the Squadron formed in Order of Battle to the Southward, in the Hope of having the Wind in from the Sea, as, by the Appearance of the Weather, was to be expected later in the Day: And, retaining the Fire-ships only, I sent Directions for the Bombs and Gallies to make Sail with the Sphynx for New York.

The Enemy being equally attentive to the same Object, no material Use could be made in an Alteration of the Wind, for a short Time, to the Southward of the East. I therefore continued the same Course the rest of the Day, under a Proportion of Sail for the Phœnix, Experiment and Pearl, having the three Fire-Ships in Tow, to keep Company with Facility: The French Ships advancing, though unequally, with all their Sail abroad.

The relative Position of the two Squadrons (about North and South from each other) remained the same on the Morning of the 11th; but by the Increase of Distance between them at Break of Day, it appeared that the Enemy had kept nearer the Wind during the Night, as their headmost Ships were then Hull down.

The Wind continuing to the East North East, and having no further Expectation of being able to gain the Advantage of the Enemy with respect to it, as before proposed, I altered the Direction of the Ships by successive Changes of the Course in the same View; or, failing still in that Attempt, to await the Approach of the Enemy, with the Squadron formed in Line of Battle ahead from the Wind to Starboard; and about Four in the Evening I made the Signal for the Ships to close to the Centre, when they shortened Sail accordingly. I had moved some Time before from the Eagle into the Apollo, to be better situated for directing the subsequent Operations of the Squadron.

The Bearing of the Enemy's Van (then under their Top-sails, between Two and Three Miles distant) was altered since the Morning from the East-North-East to South-South-East; and the French Admiral had formed his Line to engage the British Squadron to Leeward. He soon after bore away to the Southward, apparently from the State of the Weather; which, by the Wind freshening much with frequent Rain since the Morning, was now rendered very unfavourable for coming to Action with any suitable Effect.

The Wind increasing greatly that Night, and continuing violent with a considerable Sea until the Evening of the 13th, I was separated from the rest of the Squadron in the Apollo, (where I had been compelled by the Weather to remain) with the Centurion, Ardent, Richmond, Vigilant, Roebuck, and Phœnix; and, as I afterwards found, many of the other Ships had been also much dispersed.

The Apollo's Main-Mast being dangerously sprung in the Partners, which made it necessary to cut away the Top-Mast to save the Lower-Mast, and having lost her Fore-Mast in the Night of the Twelfth,

I embarked in the Phœnix, when the Weather became more moderate later in the Day, to collect the dispersed Ships, and sent the Roebuck (which had lost the Head of her Mizen-Mast) to attend the Apollo to Sandy Hook.

Having afterwards proceeded in the Centurion to the Southward, upon hearing several Guns on that Bearing in the Morning of the 15th, I discovered Ten Sail of the French Squadron, some at Anchor in the Sea, about Twenty-five Leagues Eastward, from Cape May; leaving the Centurion thereupon, in a suitable Station, to direct any of the dispersed Ships, or those which might arrive of Vice-Admiral Byron's Squadron, after me, I repaired directly in the Phœnix for the appointed Rendezvous, and joined the rest of the Squadron, this Evening, off of Sandy Hook.

The chief Damage sustained in the Squadron by the Effects of the late Gale of Wind, besides what I have before related, was confined to the Cornwall and Raisonable; the Main-Mast of the former, and Bowsprit of the last being sprung; but the Cornwall's Mast will soon be rendered serviceable. And the Thunder Bomb is still missing.

My Observations on the Ships of the French Squadron were confined solely to the Discovery of their Position. The Particulars of their Situation I have to add, were communicated by the different Commanders of His Majesty's Ships, which had been crossed earlier upon them.

The Languedoc and Tonant had lost all their Masts, the Main-Mast of the latter excepted. The Languedoc was met in that Condition in the Evening of the 13th, and attacked by the Renown with such Advantage, that the most happy Consequences might have been expected from Captain Dawson's resolute Efforts the next Morning, if the Execution of his Purpose had not been prevented by the Arrival of Six Sail of the French Squadron, which then joined the disabled Ship.

A similar Attempt, with the like Prospect of Success, was made the same Night by Commodore Hotham in the Preston, on the Tonant; and the Continuance of the Action, the next Morning, necessarily declined for the same Reason.

Neither of the Two Fifty-Gun Ships received any material Damage in those spirited Undertakings, besides the Loss of the Preston's Fore Yard, which is rendered very unserviceable.

On the 16th, the Isis was chased and engaged by a French Seventy-four-Gun Ship, bearing a Flag at the Mizen Top-Mast Head, and therefore supposed to be the Zelé. The Lords Commissioners will see in the Copy of the inclosed Report from Captain Raynor, the Event of that very unequal Contest. But it is requisite that I should supply the Deficiency of his Recital, by observing to their Lordships, that the Superiority acquired over the Enemy in the Action, appears to be not less an Effect of Captain Raynor's very skilful Management of his Ship, than of his distinguished Resolution, and the Bravery of his Men and Officers.

My chief Attention will be directed to a speedy Dispatch of the needful Repairs and Supplies in the Ships capable of being made soonest ready for Service. The Experiment has been ordered off of Rhode Island to procure Advices of the State of the Garrison at Newport; for the reducing of which the Rebels have been unavoidably left at Liberty to land any Force they may have drawn down to the adjacent Coasts, upon Rhode Island.

I am with great Consideration, &c.

HOWE.

P. S. Since my Return to this Port, I have received Letters from Captain Hawker, to acquaint me with the Loss of the Mermaid, which was forced on Shore near Senepuxen by the French Squadron, when the Enemy arrived first off of the Delaware towards the Beginning of last Month.

A List of the Squadron of His Majesty's Ships which sailed from Sandy-Hook under the Command of the Vice-Admiral the Viscount Howe, August 6, 1778.

THIRD RATE.

	Guns.	Men.	
Eagle,	64	522	Vice-Admiral the Viscount Howe.—Captains Duncan and Curtis.
Trident,	64	517	Commodore Elliot.—Captain Molloy.

FOURTH RATE.

	Guns.	Men.	
Preston,	50	367	Commodore Hotham.—Captain Uppleby.

THIRD RATE.

Cornwall,	74	600	Captain Edwards.
Nonsuch,	64	500	Captain Griffith.
Raisonable,	64	500	Captain Fitzherbert.
Somerset,	64	500	Captain Ourry.
St. Alban's,	64	500	Captain Onslow.
Ardent,	64	500	Captain Keppel.

FOURTH RATE.

Centurion,	50	350	Captain Brathwaite.
Experiment,	50	320	Captain Sir James Wallace.
Isis,	50	350	Captain Raynor.
Renown,	50	350	Captain Dawson (acting.)

FIFTH RATE.

Phœnix,	44	280	Captain Parker.
Roebuck,	44	280	Captain Hamond.
Venus,	36	240	Captain Williams.
Richmond,	32	220	Captain Gidoin.
Pearl,	32	220	Captain Linzee.
Apollo,	32	220	Captain Pownoll.

SIXTH RATE.

Sphynx,	20	160	Captain Græme.

Sloop Nautilus, 16 Guns, 125 Men, Capt. Becher.
Armed Ship Vigilant, 20 Guns, 150 Men, Captain Christian.
Fireship Strombolo, 45 Men, Captain Aplin.
Ditto Sulphur, 45 Men, Captain Watt.
Ditto Volcano, 45 Men, Captain O'Hara.
Bomb Vessel Thunder, 8 Guns, 80 Men, Captain Gambier.
Ditto Carcass, 70 Men, Lieut. Edwards (acting.)
Galley Philadelphia, Lieutenant Paterson.
Ditto Hussar, Lieutenant Sir James Barclay.
Ditto Ferret, Lieutenant O'Brien.
Ditto Cornwallis, Lieutenant Spry.

HOWE.

Copy of a Letter from Captain Brisbane to the Viscount Howe, dated Flora off Newport, July 27, 1778.

MY LORD,

I Have just now the Honor of your Lordship's Letter of the 19th Instant, in Answer to mine of the 7th by the Falcon, since which I wrote you by the Fowey on the 19th: Also your Lordship's Orders to make War upon, take or destroy all Ships of the French Nation appearing on the Coast of North America; and have given Orders, in Consequence thereof, to the Captains and Commanders of the several Ships and Vessels under my Orders.

Major-General Sir Robert Pigot acquaints me, the Batteries on Goat Island, Brenton's Neck, Dumplins, and that at the North End of the Town, are put in the best State of Defence possible for the Time, in order to prevent any hostile Intention of the Enemy.

Agreeable to your Lordship's Intimation respecting the Ships under my Orders, should the Enemy appear, and endeavour to get in, I shall take the best Precautions, according to Circumstances, for their Safety. I must observe to your Lordship, that Lieutenant Knowles, agreeable to my Directions, has got all the Transports and other Vessels into the inner Harbour, and placed the Grand Duke Storeship across the Mouth of the North Entrance, in order to prevent, as much as possible, the Enemy's destroying them: The Pigot, and Rebel Galley Spitfire, are placed at the South Entrance to answer the same Purpose; and, in case the Enemy should come

in, Lieutenant Knowles has Directions to scuttle the Transports.

As soon as I have Reason to apprehend the Enemy's Intention is not to attack this Port, I shall employ one of the advanced Ships with the Sphynx to convoy the Wood Vessels from Huntingdon to this Port, and place the Pigot Galley in her Station.

As soon as I am joined by the Ship your Lordship intends assisting me with for the Protection of the Wood Vessels, I shall employ her in convoying such of them as the General may think proper to send to Fort-Pond Bay.

In my present Situation I know no Mode of supplying the New Galley with Guns of the nearest Calibre she is constructed to bear, but by taking the 2 Eighteen-pounders out of the Rebel Galley Spitfire, which I propose doing if the Carriages will answer.

The Complements of the Pigot and Spitfire are nearly complete, and the Deficiencies shall be made up.

I have given the Surgeon of the Flora Directions to purchase Medicines for the Prisoners, agreeable to your Lordship's Directions on that Head; and have divided the Prisoners into Two Ships, separating those taken in Arms from the rest.

The 10 British Seamen brought from Boston are fit for Service; have been exchanged within the Limits of your Lordships former Directions, and distributed amongst the Ships, in order to complete their Complements: But as I have already acquainted General Sullivan, that, agreeable to your Lordship's Orders, none of the New England Prisoners could be exchanged until Restitution was made for the Circumstance of the Royal Bounty; and from a Rebel Colonel being very desirous to come to Newport to confer with General Pigot, he, as well as myself, have Reason to believe it has taken a proper Effect, from the Idea they are to be sent to England: The Conference will shew the Event.

Yesterday the Sphynx arrived from assisting in convoying the Vessels up the Sound: I intended to have sent her to cruize 10 or 12 Leagues to the Southward of Block Island, to prevent any Vessels bound to the Port of New York falling into the Enemy's Hands; but as Captain Harmood acquaints me he was informed by the People on Long Island that they have left the Hook, I shall order her to cruize between the Harbour's Mouth and Block Island, in order to give the earliest Intelligence.

As Lieutenant Andrew Congalton, First Lieutenant of the Flora, still continues incapable of Duty, from the Wound he received some Time ago, I have given an Order to Mr. Smith, Master's Mate, to act as Second Lieutenant until his Recovery, or your Lordship's Pleasure is further known.

Captain Harmood's Orders from Admiral Gambier being to return immediately, I have therefore dispatched him, with Orders to return to his Station, and forward my Letter to your Lordship as soon as possible.

I am, with great Respect,
My Lord,
Your Lordship's most obedient humble Servant,
J. BRISBANE.

*** *There being no Possibility of Printing the Whole of Lord Howe's Dispatches To-night, the Remainder will be published in a Supplemental Gazette To-morrow.*

AT the Court at St. James's, the 23d of October, 1778,

PRESENT,

The KING's Most Excellent Majesty in Council.

WHEREAS, by an Act of Parliament passed in the Tenth Year of His Majesty's Reign, intituled, " An Act to prevent the further spreading " of the Contagious Disorder among the Horned " Cattle in Great Britain," His Majesty is empowered

ered, (amongst other Things) from Time to Time, as often as he shall find it necessary so to do, by His Royal Proclamation, to be issued by and with the Advice of His Privy Council, or by His Order in Council to be published in the London Gazette, to prohibit generally, or from any particular Country or Countries, or from the Isles of Alderney, Jersey, Guernsey, or any of the Islands or Dominions belonging to Great Britain, the Importation of any Cattle, or of any Manner of Hides or Skins, Horns or Hoofs, or any other Part of any Cattle or Beast, into the Kingdoms of Great Britain or Ireland, or into any of the Islands or Dominions thereto belonging : And whereas His Majesty hath received Information, that the Distemper amongst the Horned Cattle has broke out in the Ukraine :— His Majesty doth thereupon, with the Advice of His Privy Council, find it necessary to Order, and doth hereby accordingly Order and Command, that no Horned Cattle, nor any Manner of Hides, Skins, Horns, Hoofs, or other Part of any Horned Cattle or Beast, nor any Hay, Straw, Litter, Fodder, or other Things which have been employed about Infected Cattle, or the Hides or any other Part of such Cattle, or have been in or near the Places where any such Infection hath been, and are liable to retain the same, shall be imported from any Ports or other Places within the Dominions of Russia or Poland, until His Majesty's Pleasure shall be further signified. And His Majesty is further pleased, with the Advice aforesaid, to Order, as it is hereby Ordered, that the utmost Care be taken not to permit any Entry to be passed for any Cattle, or for any Manner of Hides or Skins, Horns or Hoofs, or any other Part of any Cattle or Beast, which are already, or may hereafter be, brought from the Places aforementioned, directly or indirectly, into any of the Ports of Great Britain or Ireland, until further Order. And the Right Honourable the Lords Commissioners of His Majesty's Treasury, and the Lord Lieutenant of His Majesty's Kingdom of Ireland, are to give the necessary Directions herein, as to them may respectively appertain.

G. Chetwynd.

Navy-Office, October 23, 1778.

THE Principal Officers and Commissioners of His Majesty's Navy give Notice, that on Friday next, at Noon, they will be ready to receive Proposals for performing the under-mentioned Paviours Work at the Marine Barracks at Chatham, viz.

About 740 Yards, with hard round Purbeck Squares, not less than 5 Inches deep;

About 2800 Yards, with Kentish Raggs, from 6 to 8 Inches deep;

The Whole to be laid in screened Gravel, or sharp Sand, agreeable to such Form and Levels as shall be directed, the Contractor defraying all Expences attending the Execution of the said Works.

Victualling Office, October 26, 1778.

THE Commissioners for Victualling His Majesty's Navy do hereby give Notice, that on Monday the 30th of November next they will be ready to receive Tenders in Writing, (sealed up) and treat with such Persons as may be inclinable to undertake to furnish Sea Provisions to such of His Majesty's Ships and Vessels as may touch at Bantry Bay and Dingle in Ireland, and be in Want thereof.

The Conditions of the Contract may be seen at the Secretary's Office at this Office, or by applying to the Collectors or Chief Officers of His Majesty's Customs at Bantry Bay and Dingle in Ireland.

And all Persons who may think proper to make Tenders upon the said Occasion are desired to take Notice, that no Regard will be had to any Tender that shall not be delivered to the Board before One o'Clock on the said 30th of November next ; nor unless the Person who makes the Tender, or some Person on his Behalf, attends, to answer for him when called for.

Victualling-Office, October 15, 1778.

THE Commissioners for Victualling His Majesty's Navy do hereby give Notice, that there is Money in the Hands of the Treasurer of His Majesty's Navy to pay Interest and Non-Interest Bills, registered on the Course of the Victualling, in the Months of July, August, September, and October, 1777, in order that the Persons possessed of the said Bills may bring them to this Office, to be assigned for Payment.

NOtice is hereby given to the Officers and Company of His Majesty's Ship Andromeda, Henry Bryne, Esq; Commander, who were actually on Board at the destroying of the Angelica American Privateer, on the 30th of May, 1778, that they will be paid their respective Shares of the Bounty of Head-money, on Board, at Portsmouth, on Saturday the 31st Instant ; and the Shares then remaining unpaid will be recalled at the Fountain Tavern at Portsmouth, on the First Monday in every Month for Three Years to come.

Thomas Binsfield, of Portsmouth, Agent.

To CHRISTIAN VAN TEYLINGEN, late of the City of London, Esq.

YOU are hereby desired to take Notice, that unless you pay to Mess. Martin, Stone, Blackwell, and Foote, Bankers, in Lombard-street, London, on or before the 15th Day of December next, the Money which you owe to them, for Principal, Interest, Costs and Charges, and thereby reeem the Diamond Ring, Diamond Aigrette, Diamond Sleeveknot, the Pearls, and other Things, which, in the Year 1773, you deposited and pledged with them, on Account of a Sum of Money which they have advanced and paid for you, they will cause the said Diamonds, Pearls, and other Things, to be publickly sold, by Auction, on the 16th Day of the said Month of December, between the Hours of Twelve and Two of the Clock in the Afternoon of that Day, at the George and Vulture Tavern, in George-yard, Lombard-street, London, for the best Price that can be then gotten for the same.

October 24, 1778.

Sheffield, October 22, 1778.

NOTICE is hereby given, that the Partnership between Joshua Cawton and Son, of Sheffield in the County of York, Table Knife Cutlers, is dissolved ; and all Persons having any Demands on the said Partnership are desired to send in their Accounts to the said Joshua Cawton ; and all Debts owing to the said Partnership are to be paid to him only.

Joshua Cawton.
Benjamin Cawton.

Notice to Creditors.

ALexander Porteous, Flesher in Edinburgh, gave in a Petition to the Lord Ordinary officiating on the Bills, praying for a Sequestration of his Estate, which was awarded accordingly upon the 5th of September last ; and, upon a Minute and Recommendation from his Creditors, the Lord Westhall, Ordinary on the Bills, did, upon the 10th of October instant, nominate Alexander Ferguson, Writer in Edinburgh, to be Factor ; and appointed the Creditors to meet at Edinburgh, and within the Exchange Coffee-house there, on Wednesday the 18th of November next, at Twelve o'Clock Noon, in order to their continuing the said Alexander Ferguson Factor, or chusing another Factor, or a Trustee or Trustees, in his Place.

Alex. Ferguson.

Notice to the Creditors of Joseph Read, Bleacher, at Inglisgreen,

THAT, upon the 15th of September, 1778, the Lord Westhall, Ordinary on the Bills, did sequestrate the whole Personal Estate of the said Joseph Read, situate within the Jurisdiction of the Court ; and, upon the 1st of October in the said Year, his Lordship appointed Allan Turner, Printer at Inglisgreen, to be Factor thereon, in Terms of the late Act of Parliament concerning Insolvent Debtors, passed in the 12th Year of His present Majesty ; and further, his Lordship appointed the Creditors of the said Joseph Read to meet within John's Coffee-house in Edinburgh, on Wednesday the 18th of November next, at Twelve o'Clock at Noon, in order to their continuing the said Factor, or chusing another Factor, or a Trustee or Trustees, in his Place, in Terms of the said Statute: Of all which, Notice is hereby given by the Factor to the Creditors of the said Joseph Read, agreeable to an Appointment of Court and the foresaid Statute.

THE Creditors who have proved their Debts under a Commission of Bankrupt awarded and issued against Thomas Gladman, of Studham in the County of Hertford, Butcher, Dealer and Chapman, are desired to meet at the Swan Inn, in Market Street in the County of Hertford, on Tuesday the 10th Day of November next, in order to assent to or dissent from the Proposals then to be made of and concerning the said Bankrupt's Estate and Effects ; and on other Business relating to the said Bankrupt's Affairs.

Whereas a Commission of Bankrupt is awarded and issued forth against Samuel Williamson, late of Great Neston in the County of Chester, Check-manufacturer, Dealer and Chapman, and he being declared a Bankrupt, is hereby required to surrender himself to the Commissioners in the said Commission named, or the major Part of them, on the 16th and 17th Days of November next, and on the 8th Day of December following, at Ten o'Clock in the Forenoon on each Day, at the Coach and Horses, in Northgate-street, in the City of Chester, and make a full Discovery and Disclosure of his Estate and Effects; when and where the Creditors are to come prepared to prove their Debts, and at the Second Sitting to chuse Assignees, and at the last Sitting the said Bankrupt is required to finish his Examination, and the Creditors are to assent to or dissent from the Allowance of his Certificate. All Persons indebted to the said Bankrupt, or that have any of his Effects, are not to pay or deliver the same but to whom the Commissioners shall appoint, but give Notice to Mr. Derbyshire, Attorney, in Chester.

Whereas a Commission of Bankrupt is awarded and issued forth against Richard Radenhurst, of Birmingham, in the County of Warwick, Factor, Dealer and Chapman, and he being declared a Bankrupt, is hereby required to surrender himself to the Commissioners in the said Commission named, or the major Part of them, on the 30th Day of October instant, on the 11th Day of November next, and on the 8th Day of December following, at Three of the Clock in the Afternoon on each of the said Days, at Cooke's Coffee-house, in Cherry-street, Birmingham, and make a full Discovery and Disclosure of his Estate and Effects; when and where the Creditors are to come prepared to prove their Debts, and at the second Sitting to chuse Assignees, and at the last Sitting the said Bankrupt is required to finish his Examination, and the Creditors are to assent to or dissent from the Allowance of his Certificate. All Persons indebted to the said Bankrupt, or that have any of his Effects, are not to pay or deliver the same but to whom the Commissioners shall appoint, but give Notice to Mr. Thomas Lee, Attorney, in Birmingham.

Whereas a Commission of Bankrupt is awarded and issued forth against Samuel Du Gue, of the Parish of the Holy Trinity in the County of the City of Exeter, Merchant, and he being declared a Bankrupt, is hereby required to surrender himself to the Commissioners in the said Commission named, or the major Part of them, on the 4th and 11th Days of November next, and on the 8th Day of December next, at Four o'Clock in the Afternoon on each Day, at Swale's Wine-Cellar, in the City of Exeter, and make a full Discovery and Disclosure of his Estate and Effects; when and where the Creditors are to come prepared to prove their Debts, and at the Second Sitting to choose Assignees, and at the last Sitting the said Bankrupt is required to finish his Examination, and the Creditors are to assent to or dissent from the Allowance of his Certificate. All Persons indebted to the said Bankrupt, or that have any of his Effects, are not to pay or deliver the same but to whom the Commissioners shall appoint, but give Notice to Mess. Williams and Son, Attornies, in Exeter.

Whereas a Commission of Bankrupt is awarded and issued forth against James Kelcey, of the Parish of Wormshill in the County of Kent, Miller, Dealer and Chapman, and he being declared a Bankrupt is hereby required to surrender himself to the Commissioners in the said Commission named, or the major Part of them, on the 2d and 23d Days of November next, and on the 8th Day of December next, at Ten o'Clock in the Forenoon on each Day, at the Rose inn, in Sittingborne in the said County, and make a full Discovery and Disclosure of his Estate and Effects; when and where the Creditors are to come prepared to prove their Debts, and at the Second Sitting to chuse Assignees, and at the last Sitting the said Bankrupt is required to finish his Examination, and the Creditors are to assent to or dissent from the Allowance of his Certificate. All Persons indebted to the said Bankrupt, or that have any of his Effects, are not to pay or deliver the same but to whom the Commissioners shall appoint, but give Notice to Mr. John Hinde, Attorney, at Milton next Sittingborne in Kent.

Whereas a Commission of Bankrupt is awarded and issued forth against John Vowell, of Sherborne in the County of Dorset, Grocer, Dealer and Chapman, and he being declared a Bankrupt, is hereby required to surrender himself to the Commissioners in the said Commission named, or the major Part of them, on the 6th and 7th Days of November next, and on the 8th Day of December following, at Five in the Afternoon on each Day, at Guildhall, London, and make a full Discovery and Disclosure of his Estate and Effects; when and where the Creditors are to come prepared to prove their Debts, and at the Second Sitting to chuse Assignees, and at the last Sitting the said Bankrupt is required to finish his Examination, and the Creditors are to assent to or dissent from the Allowance of his Certificate. All Persons indebted to the said Bankrupt, or that have any of his Effects, are not to pay or deliver the same but to

whom the Commissioners shall appoint, but give Notice to Mr. Richard Edmunds, Attorney, at his Seat in the Exchequer Office of Pleas, Lincoln's-inn.

Whereas a Commission of Bankrupt is awarded and issued forth against Joseph Boyter, of the City of New Sarum in the County of Wilts, Innholder, Victualler, Dealer and Chapman, and he being declared a Bankrupt, is hereby required to surrender himself to the Commissioners in the said Commission named, or the major Part of them, on the 7th and 14th Days of November next, and on the 8th Day of December following, at Ten in the Forenoon on each of the said Days, at the House of George Webb, the Black Horse Inn, in Sarum, and make a full Discovery and Disclosure of his Estate and Effects; when and where the Creditors are to come prepared to prove their Debts, and at the Second Sitting to chuse Assignees; and at the last Sitting the said Bankrupt is required to finish his Examination; and the Creditors are to assent to or dissent from the Allowance of his Certificate. All Persons indebted to the said Bankrupt, or that have any of his Effects, are not to pay or deliver the same but to whom the Commissioners shall appoint, but give Notice to Mr. Henry Dench, Attorney, in Salisbury.

Whereas a Commission of Bankrupt is awarded and issued forth against John Rhoades the Younger, late of Hales Owen in the County of Salop, Dealer and Chapman, and he being declared a Bankrupt, is hereby required to surrender himself to the Commissioners in the said Commission named, or the major Part of them, on the 13th and 14th Days of November next, and on the 8th Day of December following, at Eleven of the Clock in the Forenoon on each of the said Day, at the House of John Caddick, called the Bush Inn, in Dudley in the County of Worcester, and make a full Discovery and Disclosure of his Estate and Effects; when and where the Creditors are to come prepared to prove their Debts, and at the Second Sitting to chuse Assignees, and at the last Sitting the said Bankrupt is required to finish his Examination, and the Creditors are to assent to or dissent from the Allowance of his Certificate. All Persons indebted to the said Bankrupt, or that have any of his Effects, are not to pay or deliver the same but to whom the Commissioners shall appoint, but give Notice to Thomas Richards, Attorney, in Dudley, Worcestershire.

The Commissioners in a Commission of Bankrupt awarded and issued against William Lee, of Chelsea in the County of Middlesex, Dealer and Chapman, intend to meet on the 17th Day of November next, at Five of the Clock in the Afternoon, at Guildhall, London, in order to make a Dividend of the Estate and Effects of the said Bankrupt; when and where the Creditors, who have not already proved their Debts, are to come prepared to prove the same, or they will be excluded the Benefit of the said Dividend. And all Claims not then proved will be disallowed.

Whereas the acting Commissioners in the Commission of Bankrupt awarded and issued against Thomas Eaton, late of the Town of Liverpool in the County of Lancaster, Mariner, Merchant, Dealer and Chapman, have certified to the Right Honourable Edward Lord Thurlow, Lord High Chancellor of Great Britain, that the said Thomas Eaton hath in all Things conformed himself according to the Directions of the several Acts of Parliament made concerning Bankrupts; This is to give Notice, that by Virtue of an Act passed in the 5th Year of His present Majesty's Reign, his Certificate will be allowed and confirmed as the said Act directs, unless Cause be shewn to the contrary on or before the 17th Day of November next.

Whereas the acting Commissioners in the Commission of Bankrupt awarded and issued against John Phillips, of Gracechurch-street, London, Grocer, have certified to the Right Hon. Edward Lord Thurlow, Lord High Chancellor of Great Britain, that the said John Phillips hath conformed according to the Directions of the several Acts of Parliament made concerning Bankrupts; This is to give Notice, that by virtue of an Act passed in the Fifth Year of His late Majesty's Reign, his Certificate will be allowed and confirmed as the said Act directs, unless Cause be shewn to the contrary on or before the 17th of November next.

Whereas the acting Commissioners in the Commission of Bankrupt awarded against Richard Watlington, of Pall-mall in the County of Middlesex, Wine-merchant, have certified to the Right Honourable Edward Lord Thurlow, Lord High Chancellor of Great Britain, that the said Richard Watlington hath in all Things conformed himself according to the Directions of the several Acts of Parliament made concerning Bankrupts; This is to give Notice, that by virtue of an Act passed in the Fifth Year of His late Majesty's Reign, his Certificate will be allowed and confirmed as the said Act directs, unless Cause be shewn to the contrary on or before the 17th Day of November next.

Erratum in the Gazette of Saturday last. In the Advertisement for a Meeting of the Creditors of Miles Barber, at the Rainbow Coffee-house, Cornhill, for Tuesday the 2d of November next, read Monday the 2d of November next.

Printed by Thomas Harrison, in Warwick-Lane. 1778.

Suggestions for Further Reading

Andrik, Todd. *Reporting the Revolutionary War: Before It Was History, It Was News* (Naperville, IL: Source Books, 2012).

Dull, Jonathan R. *The French Navy and American Independence: A Study of Arms and Diplomacy, 1774-1787* (Princeton: Princeton University Press, 1975).

Gruber, Ira D. *The Howe Brothers and the American Revolution* (Chapel Hill: University of North Carolina Press for the Institute of Early American History and Culture at Williamsburg, 1972).

Gruber, Ira D., ed. *John Pebbles' American War, 1776-1782*. Publications of the Army Records Society, vol. 13 (Stroud, Gloucestershire: Sutton Publishing, 1998).

Hattendorf, John B., ed. *Mary Gould Almy's Journal During the Siege at Newport, Rhode Island, 29 July to 24 August 1778* (Pennsauken Township, NJ: Bookbaby for the Rhode Island Society Sons of the Revolution, 2018).

Hattendorf, John B. *Newport, The French Navy, and the American Revolution* (Newport: The Redwood Press, 2005).

Londahl-Smidt, Donald M. *German Troops in the American Revolution (1): Hessen-Cassel* (Oxford: Osprey, 2021).

Mackesy, Piers. *The War for America, 1775-1783* (London: Longmans Green, & Co. 1964).

Mackenzie, Frederick. *Diary of Frederick Mackenzie, Giving a Daily Narrative of His Military Service as an Officer of the Regiment of Royal Welch Fusiliers during the Years 1775-1781 in Massachusetts, Rhode Island, and New York*. Two volumes (Cambridge: Harvard University Press, 1930).

McBurney, Christian M. *The Rhode Island Campaign: The First French and American Operation in the Revolutionary War* (Yardley, PA: Westholme Publishing, 2011).

Parkinson, Robert G. "Print, the Press, and the American Revolution" In: *Oxford Research Encyclopedia of American History.* https://doi.org/10.1093/acrefore/9780199329175.013.9.

Schroder, Walter K. *The Hessian Occupation of Newport and Rhode Island, 1776-1779* (NP: Heritage Books, 2005).

Wood, Stephen. "Lieutenant-General Sir Robert Pigot, Baronet, by Francis Coates RA, c. 1765," *Journal of the Society for Army Historical Research*, vol. 68, no. 354 (Summer 2010), pp. 111-128.

Willcox, William B., ed. *The American Rebellion: Sir Henry Clinton's Narrative of his Campaigns, 1775-1782, with an Appendix of Documents* (New Haven: Yale University Press, 1954).

Willis, Sam. *The Struggle for Sea Power: A Naval History of American Independence.* (London: Atlantic Books, 2015).

Index

In cases where an explanatory footnote is present, the page and note number are given together. For example, for an index reference on page 17 with a footnote numbered 37, the index listing is indicated as 17n37. Variant spellings in the original text have been placed in parentheses after the correct modern spelling.

About the Editor

Professor John B. Hattendorf is the Historian of the Rhode Island Society Sons of the Revolution. In addition, he also serves as Historian of the Rhode Island Society of Colonial Wars and Rhode Island Society of the Cincinnati. He is senior advisor at the U.S. Naval War College's eponymous John B. Hattendorf Center for Maritime Historical Research and Ernest J. King Professor Emeritus of Maritime History. While holding the E. J. King chair from 1984 to 2016, he was chairman of the Naval War College's Advanced Research Department, 1986-2003; chairman, Maritime History Department, and director of the Naval War College Museum, 2003-2016. As a naval officer, 1964-1973, he saw combat action while serving in destroyers during the Vietnam War. He holds degrees in history from Kenyon College (A.B., 1964), Brown University (A.M., 1971), and the University of Oxford (D.Phil., 1979; D.Litt., 2016). His numerous awards include the Anderson Medal for Lifetime Achievement from the United Kingdom's Society of Nautical Research (2017), the U.S. Navy's Distinguished Civilian Service Medal (2016) and Superior Civilian Service Medal (2006, 2016), the American Library Association's Dartmouth Medal (2007), and the Caird Medal of the National Maritime Museum, Greenwich (2000). Additionally, in 2011 the U.S. Naval War College named its Prize for Distinguished Historical Research in his honor and in 2017 its Center for Maritime Historical Research. He was inducted into the Rhode Island Heritage Hall of Fame in 2019. He is the author, co-author, editor, or co-editor of more than fifty volumes, including the four-volume *Oxford Encyclopedia of Maritime History* (2007).